There was a man that I will always remember, he had been completely cut in half at his waist. His face had a look on it, like a happy expression, his eyes were open and looking right at me. That night was painstaking long. Death did not discriminate among the passengers of Trans World Airlines Flight 800, young and old, they all died alike.

Barry R. Donadio
TWA Flight 800 First Responder

TWA FLIGHT 800 FIRST RESPONDER WITNESS ACCOUNT

The witness account of Barry R. Donadio, who responded to the TWA Flight 800 crash as a first responder during the initial moments of the disaster.

BARRY R. DONADIO

Copyright © 2013 by Barry Richard Donadio

All rights reserved under International & Pan American Copyright Conventions

ISBN-13: 978-0615878034 (Public Security LLC)
ISBN-10: 0615878032

WARNING: Explicit language and disturbing accounts are contained in this book. This account is not for persons under the age of 18.

Published by

Public Security LLC
855-589-2267
www.publicsecurityllc.com
www.publicsecurity.us

Printed in the United States of America

Preface

This account was transcribed from my original TWA Flight 800 witness account.

Many chapters are written from only what I knew in July 1996 not what I know now.

I was a 25-year-old emergency medical technician that was one of the first responders serving the East Moriches Community Ambulance on the day of the plane crash. I was there, among others to help the injured and to save lives.

And ye shall know the truth, and the truth shall make you free.

Chapters

1. THE TERRYVILLE FIRE DEPARTMENT OF NEW YORK

2. FIRST FATALITY

3. JUNE 6TH 1990 NEW JERSEY

4. INJURED

5. CENTER MORICHES FIRE DEPARTMENT NEW YORK

6. 106TH RESCUE WING NEW YORK AIR NATIONAL GUARD

7. EAST MORICHES COMMUNITY AMBULANCE NEW YORK

800. INDIDENT IN SOUTHAMPTON, NEW YORK

9. JULY 15TH 1996 SOUTHAMPTON, NEW YORK

10. WHAT THE HELL!

11. SIGNAL 27!

12. RESPONSE OF THE EAST MORICHES AMBULANCE

13. GEE THAT'S STRANGE

14. FIRST RESPONDERS AT THE TWA FLIGHT 800 CRASH

15. SURVIVORS

16. THE FIRST BOATS ARRIVE

17. THE AGONY

18. DISEMBARKING

19. HORROR

20. MAYBE WE CAN SAVE ONE

21. THE TRAUMA INFLICTED ON THE PASSENGERS OF TWA FLT. 800

22. BURNED?

23. RYDER TRUCKS?

24. INSIDE THE COAST GUARD STATION

25. WHO'S IN CHARGE HERE?

26. IMPERSONATOR

27. MYSTERIOUS PHOTOGRAPHER

28. THE EVENING COMES TO AN END

29. SALVAGE OPERATIONS

30. GABRESKI AIR NATIONAL GUARD BASE

31. THE MASS CONFUSION AT THE STROKE OF NINE

32. AIR SHOW TRADGEDY IN WESTHAMPTON

33. PRESS RELEASES

Chapter 1

THE TERRYVILLE FIRE DEPARTMENT OF NEW YORK

In April 1990, at the age of 19, I joined the Terryville fire department in New York. I became a certified interior firefighter and was also a member of the ambulance crew. I was assigned fire department badge number 253 and I was a member of engine company #2 at Terryville substation #2. My turnout gear was nothing more than firefighter boots that rolled up to your thighs, a leather traditional black firefighter's style helmet, a pair of heavy-duty leather fire retardant gloves and a firefighter's trench coat. The helmet that I was issued had the plastic flip down eye shields, the shields were high tech for that time. Many other departments did not even have that. The station was testing the tan colored firefighters trench coats, which also had full bunker pants and the latest firefighter hat that provided more protection than the current gear in use at that time. The new hat was plastic and was different shape from the traditional hat. Two of our firefighters wore that gear for test purposes.

The rest of us liked the traditional gear so we resisted the change at the beginning. At that time, style seemed to be the priority over being more protected. At some point I thought to myself, if they forced me to wear that new gear, I would request to keep my original gear because they had already taken away the fun of riding on the back step of fire trucks, and now they were going to take our identity too by changing our gear. These are just some of the small things that mattered to us firefighters back then.

Barry Donadio on a Mack class "A" pumper with open cab June 1990 Terryville Fire Department Engine Company 2, substation 2.

The Terryville Fire Department was a very well-funded, and disciplined fire department. We would respond to four to six 911 calls for help a day. Our fire commissioners projected a lot of political power and influence among the community. We were all very well trained and our certifications were always current. We had an excellent command structure for that reason we were very successful at every emergency call we responded to. The fire truck apparatus was very modern and new right down to the hose cup links. We used Mack fire trucks as our class "A" fire trucks. My engine company consisted of one open cab Mack class "A" pumper and one new state of the art closed cab pumper. I became a firefighter at the end of the age of firefighters ridding on the back step of the fire trucks, I never did ride the back step of a fire truck in my lifetime, as occupational standards, and safety administration rules (OSHA) and insurance companies put an end to all of that. Terryville had already complied with the new standard, so I did ride to calls in an open cab fire trucks, these trucks where like a convertible in fire truck form.

How fun it was being 19 years old and riding a fire truck. We would jump on the truck when a 911 call came and off we went. There was no feeling in the world like it at the time. When people needed help, we were coming to the rescue, not anyone else, just us. Sure, the police would show up, but we were needed there first to make the atmosphere safe for them to operate in at the scene. It really made us feel significant. This sense of heroism and pride was unmatched by any feeling that I had ever experienced as a young 19-year-old.

In 1990, the fire department issued me a plectron radio, it looked like a 1950's fallout shelter radio. It had the capability of being very loud, it only monitored one channel and it was the channel of the Suffolk County, New York fire communications (Firecom), when a 911 call came in, they would then alert the fire department to be able to respond.

Firecom transmitted a different set of radio beeping tones for each fire department in the county, when your fire department had a 911 call, only the plectron radios in your fire department would transmit the call to its members.

Many calls were in the middle of the night. I remember I would put the radio up loud at night because I didn't want to miss a 911 call. Sometimes we would get 3 emergency calls in the middle of the night. You never knew when the radio was going to alert you to your next emergency call to respond to.

Barry Donadio June 1990 Engine Company #2 Terryville Fire Department, N.Y.

When the radio would transmit a call in the middle of the night, it would literally make you jump out of bed. It was far louder than any alarm clock of the time. Then, after waking up you would drive to the firehouse as fast as you could and jump on a fire engine and race off to the call from there.

There were some old timers in the fire department with me that didn't even get the plectron radio when they first joined the fire department, they only knew they had a fire call when the fire department siren went off and the times it wailed told of what the call was. There was no 911 back then either. You dialed 0 for emergencies. Many of my calls in the middle of the night were false alarms because building fire alarms would go off during a storm or accidently.

For the current firefighters, because of all the false alarms that I went on, now you don't have to. Municipalities now fine building owners that keep having it happen. In old days there was no accountability for false alarms. Maybe a warning from the fire chief, that's about it.

Over the next couple of months, I remained a probationary firefighter and went to classes to complete my certificate in firematics. I responded to all types of emergencies and fires such as commercial, residential, chemical, vehicle and brush fires. I rode the ambulance and assisted senior members on ambulance responses. The entire experience was extremely rewarding, and it was my beginning as a first responder.

Chapter 2

FIRST FATALITY

Around 3am, I was awoken by the plectron radio, I already had shorts and a tee shirt on just in case of an incoming 911 call in the middle of the night. The call came over the plectron "Signal 16, 23 MVA!" What did this mean? It meant a 911 call asking for an ambulance to respond to a motor vehicle accident, and for our fire department units to assist. The heavy rescue fire truck was dispatched right away, it is only dispatched to serious accidents that may require the passengers to be cut out of the car. The heavy rescue truck was stocked with the "Jaws of Life", saws, and air bags that could lift tons of weight from a victim. We had all the newest equipment on scene that night. Terryville's station #1 had the heavy rescue truck respond from there. At least one ambulance departed from the firehouse before the heavy rescue truck arrived on the scene.

No less than 3 fire chiefs were on the scene of the call. From Terryville's station #2, where I served, a class "A" pumper was required to respond in. We were assigned to protect the firefighters on the scene from fire, while they worked to free the driver. My response to this call was like my response to many other calls. After jumping out of bed from hearing the plectron go off, I started driving my brown 1978 Chevy, Nova, we were issued a blue dashboard light to clear the traffic in front of us, this was so we could get to the firehouse faster. I came into the back parking lot, I left my keys in the ignition, and then I had to find my firehouse key for the back door of the building, I got in there and opened the back bay door. I did this so other firefighters didn't have to use a key to get in. I ran to my turn out gear that was hanging on a rack near the fire truck. I always put my boots on first, then my trench coat. I grabbed my hat and my gloves. Then, got on the open cab class "A" Mack pumper. It was exciting and we felt unbeatable. It was such an incredible high to race in a fire truck to rescue people and save lives.

The driver pulled the fire truck just outside the bay doors of the firehouse. We stood by for other firefighters running in and mounting on the pumper. We waited only seconds, which seemed like long moments of holding your breath. The top fire truck light bar was on and rotating with spectacular red and white lights. The strong colors of a fire truck light bar struck our faces while we were in the back of the truck. The fire truck radio was loud, and the driver was already communicating with others on the scene, he stated that we were about to depart. The fire truck officer mounted into the front passenger seat. He would be responsible for the siren, communications, accountability of the riders and leading the firefighters on his truck.

We had a driver and officer in the front, and four of us firefighters in the back of the cab. The pumper began its roll to the street with the wail of a siren, we were off with fury! We had a full complement of firefighters on board with at least 500 gallons of water for the fight ahead if needed. We were hungry for the action, and we were in an immortal state of mind. The call was only about 1 mile and a half away. The American flag on the truck was waving in the dark night and the wind was hitting our faces. Each pulse of the red and white emergency lights brought more excitement to us. I think we got to the scene in about 60 seconds. We came into the scene a bit fast. Until that night, I did not know a fire truck could come to such an abrupt stop. I nearly fell out of the truck, thus the reason for all class "A" pumpers to have closed cabs today.

We all jumped off our truck and pulled the inch and three-quarter hose off the side of our pumper. We then took an overwatch position to the rescue operations of a terrible car accident. There was no need to hook up to a fire hydrant because of our 500 gallons already on the truck. We always tried to have at least 3 firefighters on one hose line, the nozzle person, number 2 person, and number 3 were about four feet back from number 2 person.

Sometimes we had the luxury of having a fourth person on the fire hose. Number 4 would be making sure the hose was not kinked and would take the place of number 3 person in case they need to move up and take the place of number 2 or the nozzle person.

I must have been the number 3 or 4 person on the hose for this call, there was no time to look or stare when you were setting all this up. Once in place, we had time to observe the scene, by that time the heavy rescue firefighters had already cut the roof from the red car. This revealed the driver who was trapped. She was a young lady about 19 or 20 years old. She had driven directly head on into a large tree at about 60 miles per hour. The car simply crumpled around the tree with her in it. There were certainly enough personnel on the scene to help, probably about 20. This gave my pumper crew the opportunity to just simply watch while we held the firehose. I was new to these types of sights, so I was the biggest violator of staring that evening. The emergency medical technician (EMT) and fire chief were in the car with the victim talking to her. It took a long time to get her out of the car. I could not hear what she was saying, but she was talking, and she was conscious when I first arrived.

The problem was that the dashboard of the car had pushed in on her. It trapped her in the car, and we could not get her out quickly, but we knew we would eventually.

There was a concern that the dashboard was the only thing holding her blood pressure up. The loss of blood circulation to the lower extremities caused a big problem. When you release the dashboard from a victim that is trapped like that, all the blood rushes to the lower extremities rapidly, this sometimes causes immediate death because you suddenly have no blood pressure. This was the case for the victim that night. After being on the scene for about 45 minutes we lifted the dashboard from her legs, she immediately lost consciousness and her life as the dashboard was lifted from her. The hospital was only 5 minutes away, a desperate attempt was made to just get her on the ambulance as fast as possible and get to the hospital. No CPR attempt was made from the wreckage to the ambulance, as this was the more practicable choice. It took many rescuers to lift her out of the car and get her to the ambulance. This added precious moments to an effort that was unfortunately doomed. My pumper crew stood helpless because our job was to protect them from fire. All we could do was observe and be ready to act if fire presented itself.

As she was lifted out of the car, I saw that her foot had been completely broken, and it was turned around from its normal position. Her young eyes were open, and she presented no signs of life. The rescuers carried her into the ambulance and started CPR, the doors closed, and the emergency lights were on. The ambulance paused for a moment, after about 30 seconds of hesitation, the ambulance sped off as fast as an ambulance could go. It made it to the nearest hospital, but she was gone. I cared for the victim, and I prayed for her, that was all I could do.

The next day was yet another set of 911 calls that we would respond to. It was like nothing happened the night before. I would move on from the sights of that night and trade them for many more sights to come.

Chapter 3

JUNE 6TH 1990 NEW JERSEY

June 6th, 1990, was a hot summer day that yielded a horrific event. I was still firefighter of Terryville fire department in New York. On that day I was in New Jersey, I was there to process from the Army National Guard into the Army Reserve. I was at the Newark, New Jersey Army MEPS center for in processing. After the day was over, the recruiter picked me up and we were driving back to New York, as he drove me, we talked and enjoyed ourselves. We were driving along a 3-lane highway, and as we continued, I noticed an accident on the other side of the highway. The car in the accident had been hit in the back. The man who hit it appeared to be drunk. The car that he hit burst into flames on impact. There was a young lady in her early 20s that was in the other car that he hit. Somehow, she was still in the vehicle when I noticed it was on fire. I yelled out: "Sarge! There is someone in that car! Stop!" The recruiter pulled over and I got out of the car. We stopped about 50 yards past the scene of the accident, I had to run to get to the accident scene. In my mind I thought that I could handle this and save her.

I was thinking that I was going to get to the car and pull her out. As I ran to the car and arrived, I noticed that the car was already filled with black smoke. I could not see the occupant; the victim's car was (Redacted).

I found it odd that the back windows to this four-door car were half open, but the front windows were closed. It gave just enough ventilation for the fire to spread rapidly through the driver's compartment. There was still a chance I could save her. I observed a young college aged girl standing outside the victim's passenger side door. She was screaming for the victim to get out. They were best friends. The victim was following this girl somewhere when an alleged drunk driver had struck her.

I questioned in my mind why this girl just didn't reach in the car and rip her friend out before the fire spread. I think she believed the car would explode, so she remained paralyzed and didn't rescue her friend. An intense heat confronted me upon my arrival to the burning car, the trunk portion of the car was completely engulfed in flames. I knew that she could only survive a few breaths after taking in the black poisonous hot smoke. I rushed in and made my move to rescue her. My plan was to hold my breath, open the door and dragged her out. No one was trying this; I was the only one there attempting a rescue. I cautiously moved in, and when I got only within a foot of the driver's side door handle, I had to retreat. All the hair on my arm burned and shriveled up. At that moment I remembered that I was a firefighter and that I had to get her out. I made my second attempt to rescue her.

My second attempt at a rescue only ended in retreat due to the most extreme heat. I saw a man coming to me with a very small fire extinguisher that you would find in your kitchen. I ran to him and said: "Can I try that?" He said: "yes!" He started to say something to me and then stopped. The look he gave me was basically in disbelief that I was going to try to do anything with that tiny extinguisher, but I had to try. I attacked the fire through the back window with the fire extinguisher, it was completely ineffective. At about that same time, a separate brave man brought a baseball bat and began hitting the front windshield with it, he didn't even crack the glass. I cheered him on and told him: "Keep hitting it!" Then when that didn't work, I said: "Hit the driver's window!" I knew that this window was thinner than the front windshield and we may be able to make a final attempt at a rescue. I was thinking the driver must have been dead already because it was just so hot. I was trying to get the body recovered for the family, so it would not be destroyed by fire. To this point the entire event lasted only about 90 seconds.

The failure of the rescue began to set in as the belligerency of the flames destroyed rescue. The front seat with driver inside was now engulfed in flames. All was lost. The young girl who had been screaming next to her friend's car the entire time was now in hysteria and in need of help. I watched my hopes of saving a young lady go up in orange flames. Disappointment in myself kicked in, fast. I felt like this was my failure and my fault. I have suffered with the victim because of her life being lost. I was shocked that I could not get her out of that car alive.

Elements of the New Jersey police forces began to show up to the scene. I notified the first one of them on scene that a body was in the car. The flames continued to have its way unrestricted. The fire grew more intense. The brave local New Jersey fire department arrived on scene and their response was extremely fast, but simply after the fact. They attacked the fire and gallantly did their duty.

The fire was now extinguished. No less than 200 on lookers observed the victim from a distance. Traffic stopped on this major highway in both directions to observe the spectacle. The burnt smell of the victim overtook me. Her burnt flesh, smelled exactly like burnt Italian sausage to me.

The smoke cleared revealing what remained of the victim. There was nothing much left of her. There was only a skeleton with black charred flesh still attached to it. The fire burnt her mostly to the bone. You could not tell if she were man or woman. I looked at her head and could see her cranium. At that moment, you could smell her burnt flesh even more. My job was done. I got out of there.

I still do not know her name. She probably knows mine because I have prayed for her many times in my life. I remembered this attempted rescue long time after the event. I made myself a promise that I would rather die trying to get someone out, then allowing them to be burned alive. My decision had been made that if I were placed in the same situation again, I would sacrifice myself for the victim.

On June 22, 1997, 6 years later, this promise would be put to the test.

Chapter 4

INJURED

On December 17, 1990, I had completed my training in firematics and received my diploma, I was no longer a probationary firefighter. I was now twenty years old, and I had gained some respect of my fellow firefighters, because of my response to calls and experience that I gained. In those times, I was home all day and responded to 911 calls when most of the other firefighters were at their day jobs. One time, while still on probation, I responded to a very dangerous basement fire in a house. Basement fires are most scary to a firefighter because the potential to be trapped without escape is high. I was the number 2 person on the hose that day when we knocked down the fire and were relieved by other firefighters in the basement. The nozzle person and I stepped outside. All the other firefighters noticed I had been in the thick of it all, and this created some acknowledgment from my peers. Another incident was when a fierce house fire had torn through its upstairs bedroom late at night.

There were no occupants in this fire, but the homeowner's dog fell prey to the blaze. On this call, I was in the right place at the right time. I was the number 2 person on the hose. We went in thinking that there could be people in the house. We kicked in the front door and right of the stairs to where the fire was. We made a left turn at the top of the stairs and kicked in the bedroom door. A wave of heat hit us as the nozzle person watered down what was left of the room ceiling with a strait stream of water. Most of ceiling was gone and we were looking at the stars in the sky from the bedroom. It was an exciting fire at first. We didn't need to wear our scott pack. A scott pack is a mask hooked up to compressed air bottle that may last 15 minutes, at best. After those 15 minutes are up, you can die from suffocation, unless of course you can jump out a window or something to get out of there in order to breath. It was a nice, ventilated fire with all the smoke going into the sky and not into our lungs.

We knocked down the fire fast, this created a steam that began to burn and suffocate us. The nozzle man and I paused to put on our masks that were dangling from our gear. We could not breath, the steam was suffocating us from only taking one breath. I don't think the number 3 firefighter on the hose even saw us struggling. I got my mask on and took a few gasps while choking and nearly vomiting.

At this same time, the nozzle man put his mask on and took a huge breath, I guess he took most of the bad smoke and steam in his lungs before me. What he and I did not realize was that his mask collected paint chips and water inside it, so when the nozzle man took his first breath, he breathed in nothing but paint chips and water.

I was unaware of what the cause was, but I saw him get weak in the knees and look like he was dying. I had to get him out of there and fast. I had no idea what was wrong. He was still able to stand, but only like a completely disoriented drunk. We abandon the hose and number 3 man on the hose looked at me confused he never saw what happened. I yelled at him: "Take the hose! I have to get him out of here!" As I passed the number 4 man, I yelled: "Get up there!" The number 3 man and number 4 man took the nozzle and number 2 position that we had vacated. Us four remaining firefighters were the only ones in the burning house while there about 25 more firefighters outside. I was stumbling down the stairs with my injured nozzle man.

There was still a true danger that the fire could reignite and kill the others inside. The rescuers outside still had no idea that we had a firefighter down and in need of medical attention. "Where t is my radio?", I thought to myself. I could call for help! "Oh!", I said. He has it and it is all wrapped up around him. I was thinking: "Let me get him out of here!" The injured nozzle man and I fell down the last 4 stairs of the staircase. I picked him up and violently pushed away the front door, which was flapping in the wind. We made it to the front stoop. We cleared from the doorframe. There was a pause as the entire fire department stopped and stared for that split second, they stared hard. It felt like an entire minute. This was their first knowledge of what had occurred, and they were shocked. About 5 of other firefighters grabbed my injured nozzle man from my arms and whisked him into an ambulance. We always had an ambulance standing by in case someone got hurt. The ambulance sped off to the hospital. I don't even think they knew what was wrong with him until they were already down the road. It all happened that fast.

When the ambulance left, I turned around and went back in the house. I went up the stairs to help the other two inside.

The levelheaded fire chief sent in more reinforcements and ordered me to stay outside because I had enough. I was disappointed at the order, but I followed it. It was like a tag team in wrestling match. When you had enough, you had enough. You had to sit out. The fire chief was correct to do what he did. Since my beginning with the Terryville fire department, I had become quite experienced and handled scores of fires and medical emergencies.

Brush fires were intriguing; we would drive right into them with a pickup truck type fire truck. Now that was exciting at the time. It could also get a bit dangerous. I was the passenger in the pickup truck, and we were driving through a large field to get to a big brush fire, we hit this huge hole and I broke the fire truck windshield with my head. Thank God, I had my helmet on. I didn't feel a thing. We put out the fire and laughed it all off.

On January 25th, 1992, at 5:47 am the plectron radio went off. I did my usual routine and responded to Terryville's fire station #2. The call was confirmed as a working commercial building fire, your heart races and the thoughts fly though your head. Could I be killed on this call? The call was on the other side of town, so the driver of the fire truck took extra liberties to get us there faster than usual.

This was at risk to all of us, but this is what we loved to do. Shouts on the radio from other firefighters on the scene, confirmed that the fire was out of control and serious. The fire engine officer ordered me to dismount and dress the fire hydrant when we got to the scene.

This means that our pumper would stop at the fire hydrant, and I would hook up the hose to fight a long battle with the fire. On went my scott pack, while we were in the back of the cab of the speeding fire truck. It was going to be a wild call and we knew it. Another challenge we faced was the cold, it was one of the coldest nights that I have ever seen. The wind was blowing and freezing our faces, but I was ready as we rolled to the nearest fire hydrant to the burning buildings. I jumped out of the fire truck and pulled the hose off it, to hook up to the fire hydrant. I quickly wrapped the hose around the hydrant and then the truck officer yelled: "Go! Go! Go!" The truck sped off to the fire leaving me at the fire hydrant. The fire truck only had 500 gallons on it, which goes quick in a large fire. If I didn't hook up the hose to the hydrant quickly, the other firefighters would be out of water and could die.

I first opened the large hydrant cover to make sure the neighborhood kids didn't put anything in it to impede the flow of water. Next, I used the fire hydrant wrench to open the flow of water and check that the hydrant is working and has good pressure. Out gushed water with great flow. I was shaking from the cold. Then I shut off the water. I screwed the hose cup link up to the hydrant; tighten it with the hydrant wrench.

Then, I used the hydrant wrench to slowly release water to the pumper waiting for water resupply about 250 yards away.

If you open the water valve on the fire hydrant too fast, it can destroy the fire truck and hose lines. This is called water hammer. The excitement was so intense. The mix of cold and excitement influenced me to open the fire hydrant a little fast. This caused one of the older firefighters to yell at me: "Water hammer! God dam it!" I was very embarrassed. I was spared because it caused no damage, and all was well. That was forgotten as the fire raged out of control. After dressing the hydrant, I ran to the pumper, and began to pull hose off the truck. I did relieve a few kinks in the hoses. Any water that hit the ground that night, turned to ice in moments, there was a spot you could ice skate in the parking lot that dripped from our hoses. We requested mutual aid from Setauket, Port Jefferson, and Mount Sinai fire departments.

Upon their arrival, we were 100 firefighters strong. I continued pulling more hose off the truck until I slipped on the ice and fell violently, flat on my back. I knew I was hurt right away. Being 21 years old at that time, I was more flexible.

I got up slowly and was now soaked. I was frozen, with the wind knocked out of me. The walls caved in on the building and the fire got the better of the structure. It was later labeled as suspicious and placed under investigation by the police arson squad. I went home after that call and the next day I went to the hospital.

It felt weird at the spot of my right upper back. I filed a workman's compensation case, being young, I never showed up to the hearing. Life was good being a Terryville firefighter. I didn't want compensation for any injury at the time. The injury to my back from that night still gives me discomfort even today.

Chapter 5

CENTER MORICHES FIRE DEPARTMENT NEW YORK

By February 15th, 1993, I had joined the Center Moriches Fire Department engine company #2 in New York, this is because I had moved out of Terryville's fire district and now lived in Center Moriches. If you moved, you simply joined the fire department where you lived. The problem was that the new fire department made you a probationary fireman all over again, so even with all my prior experience, I was considered a new firefighter or what was called a "Probie".

The Center Moriches Fire Department was considerably different than the Terryville Fire Department. It was much less funded and simply more laid back. The opposite of a militaristic culture and much more family orientated. The town was old fashioned and so were we. The fire trucks were much older.

It was a little more dangerous to be a firefighter in Center Moriches than in Terryville, this is because Center Moriches fire district did not have fire hydrants everywhere. We had to bring a fire truck water tanker with us everywhere. If you ran out of water in a fire you were dead for the most part.

We had an old 1970's yellow class "A" pumper. It worked like a charm and the engine was very loud, you could hear it from across town when it drove. Not what you would expect from a fire truck in full-service status. The sound of the engine had the ability to hurt your ears if it was pushed too hard while you were riding in the back of it. It was just a little tight to sit in. The older fire trucks were smaller than they are today.

Firefighter Barry Donadio, Center Moriches Fire Department, New York 1994

That fire truck was nearly a liability to use on calls, but it always got the job done. It did work and we used the heck out of it. What a difference between the two departments. Make no mistake about it, the Center Moriches Fire Department, was equally effective. The members of the Center Moriches Fire Department were also brush fire experts. We had a World War II troop carrier truck that was painted red. We used it to drive into brush fires, it had 3 small fire hoses on it. What a blast it was to ride in the back of it!

The firefighters at Center Moriches were from a very long line of other Center Moriches firefighters.

Fire trucks of the Center Moriches Fire Department in 1994

I was issued badge number 113 and had the same type of turnout gear as the Terryville. The Center Moriches was not accepting the newer turnout gear and only used the traditional gear that we all loved. Just about every truck in the inventory was open cab. Center Moriches simply did not have the funding to comply with any OSHA standards at that time. I think the only truck we had at the time with a closed cab was our new heavy rescue truck.

It was a red beauty. For some reason, in the 1970's Center Moriches went with the yellow paint on their trucks but were now heading back to red again. Red being fireman's favorite color It was great to keep putting off getting closed cabs, so we could still be riding in those open cab trucks. The people from Center Moriches Fire Department never seemed to leave that town. They joined that fire department generation after generation. At first, I stuck out a bit as an outsider from the west of Long Island.

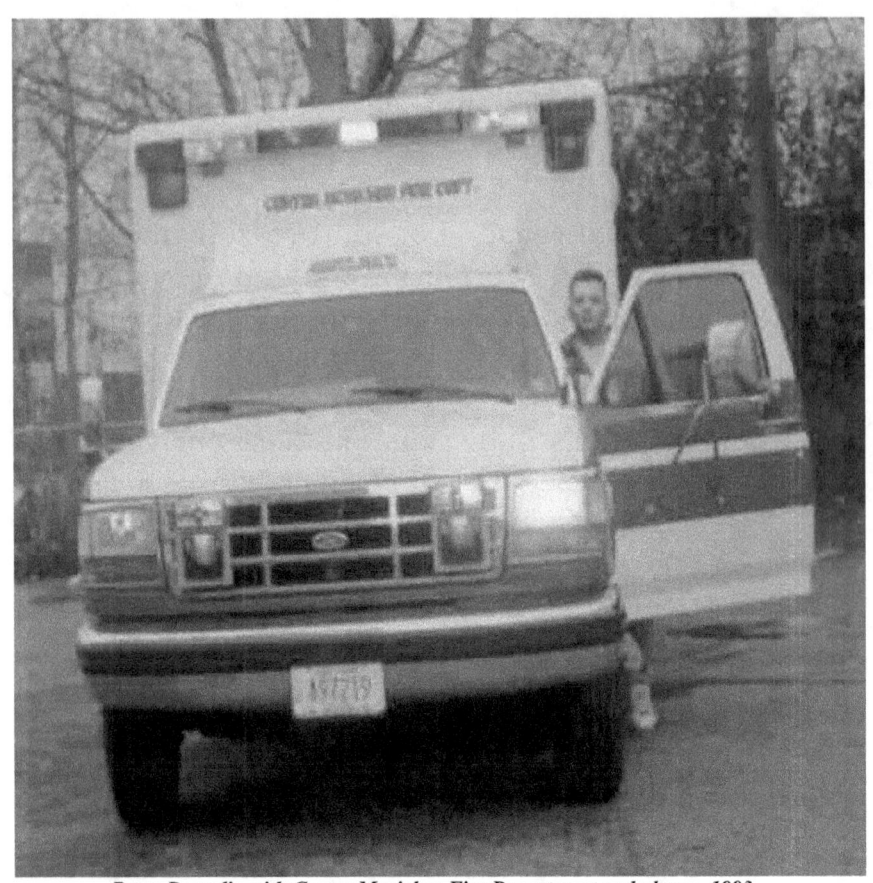
Barry Donadio with Center Moriches Fire Department ambulance, 1993

I only served in the Center Moriches Fire Department for one year and three months, but it seems to me to have been longer. From February 15th, 1993, to December 31st, 1993. I responded to no less the 37 ambulance 911 calls for service and 56 fire department 911 calls for service. From January 1st, 1994 to May 28th, 1994, I had responded to at least 17 fire calls and 32 calls for the ambulance. Not a bad run for a fire department that had about half the calls Terryville got per year. I was quite active in the department, and I loved to serve the community.

I was certified to drive both Center Moriches Fire Department ambulances. To get your certification as a driver, you had to demonstrate that you could drive the ambulance in a figure eight, but in reverse. Sounds easy but try it without looking back over your shoulder and only using mirrors. I passed the driving test, but it wasn't easy.

Center Moriches was a big player in many of the brush fires in the area. The eastern Long Island fire departments like Center Moriches had put some funding toward dealing with the threat from brush fires. These departments all had the old WWII troop carriers as brush fire trucks. There was effective because they could drive deep into the woods and knock down trees to get to the fire. Departments like Terryville, which were more suburban, had only pickup trucks as a brush fire truck. They would easily get stuck off road.

Barry Donadio with Center Moriches Fire Department brush fire truck 1993

Barry Donadio, Center Moriches Fire Department while training at the Yapank, New York fire academy 1993

There were a few times when we would respond to other fire districts to help them put out a brush fire. I think the largest one I went to as a firefighter had about 40 fire departments fighting on that brush fire. In our brush truck, we had a driver and an officer in the front. In the back you had two people on the water hoses and a tail gunner water hose.

You would be in real danger of the brush fire blowing over you and wiping out your truck and crew.

At a fire I remember the sun was blacked out in broad daylight from the smoke. We had driven our truck right into the flames. We choked a bit and our eyes burned. After a minute or so, you were fine and ready to fight some more.

Another fire remains in my memory. A tank blew up at a nursery and it ignited 5000 gallons of fuel oil. This happened very instantaneous. I happened to be at the firehouse when the explosion occurred. One firefighter was outside and heard the explosion. He ran in to tell the rest of us. We leaped up and ran to the truck bay.
No one knew what happened, but we knew it was bad. We still had not got the call from 911 at the time.

I quickly put my boots on, jacket on, and my hat on my head. I was holding my gloves and we jumped on the yellow old 1970s era class "A" pumper. We were all mounted before the driver even started the fire truck. He started the fire truck up and black smoke came from its exhaust into the truck bay.

The top red and white bar on the fire truck was on and I was feeling ready. It was broad day light, and the town was scrambling.
Many heard the explosion and saw smoke from the explosion. They did not know what it was. The truck bay door opened and the Center Moriches fire department first due truck began its roll out with me on it.

The fire truck broke the threshold of the bay door of the fire house. We were then off to the scene.

We began to roll off the firehouse apron. The fire truck engine roared loudly. We made a right turn out of the main firehouse. The wail of both trucks on board sirens and our air horn drew everyone's attention. They were all on at one time and it sounded like there were 3 trucks instead of one. We rolled down Main Street at full throttle. The class "A" pumper engine was loud and ear piercing. It sounded like the engine would cease. As we cleared passed some trees driving down Main Street, I noticed a mushroom cloud. It looked like a small nuclear bomb went off. There were people running and driving away from the mushroom cloud and we were driving to it. The truck radio blurted out the 911 call only seconds after our departure from the firehouse. We were following the mushroom cloud, but now we knew where exactly to drive and what we had when dispatch told us.

When I observed the cloud, I got a little concern for what lay ahead. I immediately started putting on my scott pack and began to mentally prepare for arriving on the scene.

I figured there would be many casualties and I knew how that looked. You just never get used to it and you brace yourself for the sights you will see. There had to be many dead after such an explosion. After a moment of mental preparation, I was ready. Other Center Moriches fire trucks were racing and a half-mile behind us, but we would be there first. Our fire truck sirens wailed, as we got closer to this tragedy. I could hear on the radio that fire communications had already begun requesting other fire departments to respond into the scene to assist Center Moriches. Good call on their part. In all, the fire departments of Manorville, Mastic, Mastic Beach, Brookhaven, Yapank, Eastport, and East Moriches had responded into our aid. The bonds we built between brother departments were unbreakable. Some fire departments got along and had bonds for over 100 years.

There were also cases where some departments hated each other and would skip over them when requesting aid.

Even if they were the adjoining district, I observed that in my time. In the old days, the fire departments on Long Island would brawl at a scene if they felt that the fire call was in their district and not in the opposing fire departments district.

There was also talk of all-out war between some New York fire departments. All this was the ugly side of the fire department culture in New York leading up to when I became a firefighter.

Rolling into the scene of this disaster, we had observed that the fuel oil had channeled itself around the greenhouses at the nursery.

It was all ablaze and uncontrolled. Our crew acted swiftly upon our arrival.

I believe we pulled the 1 inch and 3/4 line. This fire was ragging as we pulled the hose in for our attack. I was thinking to myself: "We got this fire beat". We positioned into place and moved towards the flame. I was the number 2 person on the hose. The hose was not yet charged with water, so we were very vulnerable. The driver of the pumper had to dismount and prime the pump and send the water to the hose. Sometimes, we were faster than him and we are waiting with an empty hose. There was a moment of pause as we stood there waiting for the water to fill the hose, but there was no time to waste. The fire was staring at us also. It was trying to devour its prey, which was us. We were concern for another explosion that may kill us all unless we could get some water on this fire fast. We were still the only fire truck there and we desperately needed water on this fire. Somehow, one of the old firefighters showed up on the scene next to us. Us younger guys felt reassured when the older guys we there.

There were always some old firefighters that were too old to fight fires but were still members of the fire department. They normally directed traffic at fires and joined the fire police company of the fire department. Their ages usually ranged anywhere from 60 to as high as 100 years old! They were always full of knowledge.

They sometimes seemed to be a cranky, but we listened when they spoke. The empty hose in our hands was about to be charged with water.

To not waste one second, the nozzle person already had the nozzle open before the water was even in the hose. "Hurry, hurry!" I thought to myself. I began to sweat profusely. In a fast action, the water violently rushed down the hose, out the nozzle and on to the flames.
This caused a tremendous ignition of more flames and we almost burnt ourselves up bad. "What? Water on flames and we almost killed ourselves", I thought. The old fireman next to us started yelling at us, "Foam, foam, foam!" the nozzle man looked back at me and then we got it in our brains. The old fireman was right! This was a chemical fire that required foam to mixed in the water to extinguish the fire. The water we shot at it only created a chemical reaction that made more fire. The foam was needed so it could suffocate the flames. We shut down the hose and watched the fire rage. The driver signaled over to us, and we opened the nozzle again. The most beautiful white foam I have ever seen began to flow out of our nozzle and put those flames to sleep.

At about that time, the entire Center Moriches fire department was engaged in a combat with this fire. Our brother fire departments rolled into our rescue, and it was an easy day after that.

It sounds easy, but we were not quite sure if we would die that day or not. Especially on the way to the fire when we didn't know what was ahead. As for the casualties went, there was not even one. There are such things as miracles and this day was one of them. I still have no idea how not one person was killed or injured during that event.

By May 28th, 1994, I left the Center Moriches Fire Department and later joined the community ambulance that has exposed me to an event that caused me to write this book.

Chapter 6

106TH RESCUE WING NEW YORK AIR NATIONAL GUARD

After publication review, the United States Government authorized release of information regarding my duties at the 106th Rescue Wing:

Staff Sergeant / Investigator / Team Leader
Feb. 1994 / Mar. 2002

On February 24th, 1994, I joined the 106th Rescue Wing. I was a member of the Security Police force on Gabreski air base. On May 1st, 1995, I obtained a full-time active-duty position there. I held the rank of Staff Sergeant in a full-time active-duty position. I conducted law enforcement operations and provided protection to U.S. Air Force priority resources. On July 16th, 1997, I was appointed a Security Police Investigator. The investigative duties included. criminal investigation, investigation of violation of the Uniformed Code of Military Justice (UCMJ), investigation of suspicious circumstances, terrorist threat assessments, analysis of criminal intelligence and conducting security surveys for United States Air Force resources. I served as the Team Leader of the Emergency Services Team (EST)(SWAT). This team was an elite, highly armed and trained tactical team consisting of 6 members. This team operated in support of the space shuttle recovery team, U.S. presidential visits, and September 11th, 2001. After the 9/11 attacks, I was the Team Leader of a contingency of Security Police Officers that consisted of squad of Security Police personnel consisting of four full-time and eight part-time members.
were designated to protect Air Force alert aircraft. I was member of the protective detail that protected Air Force One and Air Force Two. My deployments included Operations Northern Watch, Constant Vigil, and Noble Eagle. I was received multiple awards for accomplishments, as well as the Air Force Commendation medal. In 1997, I was selected as Airman of the Year at my airbase.

Due to USAF regulations, I am unable to release any copies of my investigations recorded on official investigation form (DD Form 1569)

Barry Donadio, December 1996, 106th Security Police, Gabreski Airbase, Westhampton Beach, New York

*Barry Donadio 106th Rescue Wing Security Police
Gabreski Airbase, Westhampton Beach, New York*

**Barry Donadio, 106th Rescue Wing Security Police
Westhampton, New York July 9, 1994**

**Barry Donadio at the front gate of Gabreski Airbase, New York
106th Rescue Wing Security Police**

Chapter 7

EAST MORICHES COMMUNITY AMBULANCE NEW YORK

After publication review, the United States Government authorized release of information regarding my duties at the East Moriches Community Ambulance.

Emergency Medical Technician Certified
Jul. 1996 / 2011

As an Emergency Medical Technician, I was one of the first arriving EMT's to the scene of TWA Flight 800 crash in 1996. I also served the East Moriches Ambulance in New York, the United States (Redacted) and the (Redacted). Additionally, I provided emergency medical assistance to countless people throughout my career.

I then joined the East Moriches community ambulance. While serving as an ambulance driver and aid person on the ambulance, I attended school to become certified as an Emergency Medical Technician.

On June 13th, 1996, I was certified as a New York State Emergency Medical Technician with defibrillator endorsement. Back then you needed the endorsement even to use the defibrillators that today we all have access to in public venues.

The certification was EMT-D. There was also EMT-B for "basic". They were not allowed to use the defibrillator.

You also could become an EMT-I for intermediate. They were authorized to start an IV on a patient. Then if you have 3 years to devote for school, you could become a Paramedic. They could do everything mentioned and administer drugs and do advance airway interventions on a patient. Back then, an EMT-D was a respectable certification. You only needed a minimum of EMT-B to legally respond to a 911 call in the ambulance.

Then in 1996, the East Moriches community volunteer ambulance was a tight knit group of only 29 members, including myself. It had 2 van type box ambulances and 2 first responder vehicles.

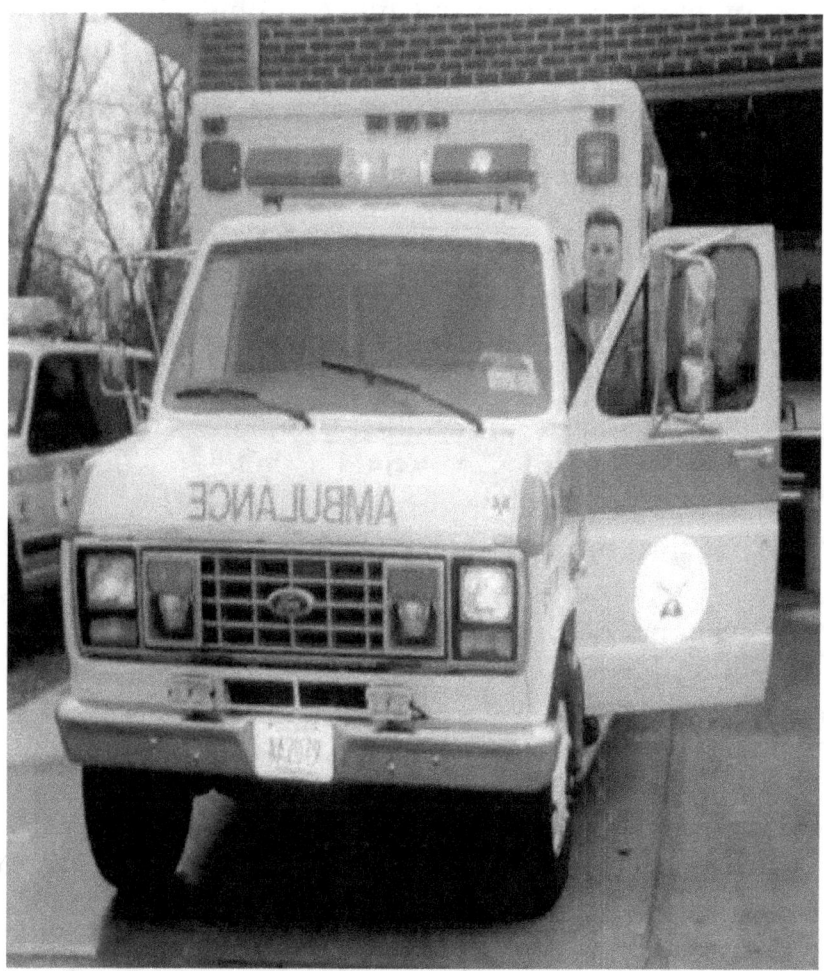
Barry Donadio, East Moriches Community Ambulance, New York 1996

One ambulance was white, and orange and the other ambulance was white and blue. One first responder vehicle was a small truck and the other was a blue car that looked like a police car. The orange first responder truck stayed at the ambulance garage and the other first responder car went home with any EMT that signed it out for the day to use. The purpose of the first responder vehicles was if there was only an EMT that showed at the garage for a 911 call, they could head down to the call themselves. Because we had such a low number of members, there were many times we would have to give up the 911 call to another jurisdiction because we could not staff the ambulance for the call. In the least bit, we could send down an EMT in the first responder vehicle and stabilize the patient until other East Moriches members showed up with the ambulance or an adjoining district responded to our call for mutual aid. We had no plectron radios by that time. We all had the most advanced pagers to receive ambulance calls over the pagers.

The East Moriches Community Ambulance was a separate entity from the East Moriches fire department. Although the ambulance garage was across the street from the firehouse, they were two different organizations and were not interchangeable. Both had a great working relationship. The Terryville and Center Moriches fire departments were all fire and ambulance combined in one and not separate. In East Moriches and many other districts, they were separate. The East Moriches firefighters could not ride or drive our ambulances and we could not go in their fire apparatus.

Emergency Medical Technician *Barry Donadio,*
East Moriches, New York 1996

Emergency Medical Technician Barry Donadio, East Moriches Ambulance first responder unit. New York 1996

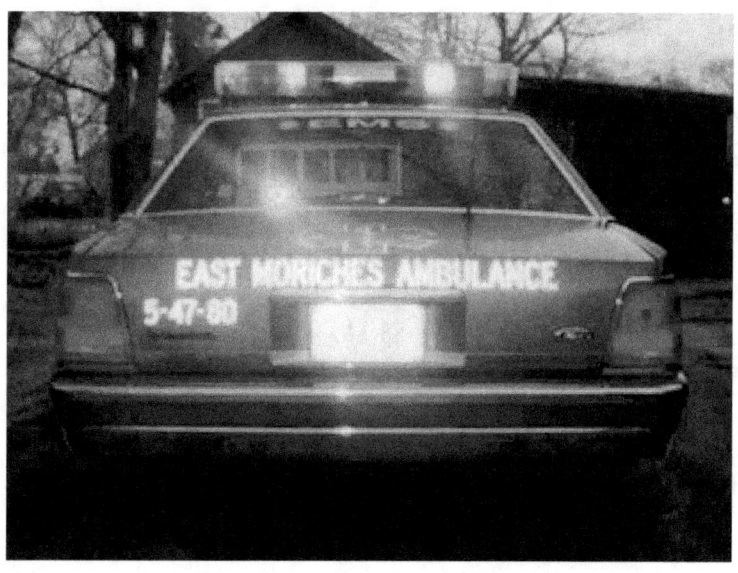

The East Moriches ambulance district was, a little bit in the sticks. There was not much in East Moriches. We had some farms and houses. There was also a small Coast Guard station, but we rarely heard from them. Our ambulance not only was responsible for East Moriches, it also covered the villages of Eastport and Speonk. By fire department standards, it was lacking a lounge, but it did its job. There was a book you signed into when you went on a call to receive credit for going. This was so they could keep track of who went on what ambulance calls. The East Moriches ambulance company also had a storefront location about a mile down the road on Montauk Highway. This is where meetings were held, and administrative functions were conducted. There were no emergency response vehicles stationed at the storefront at the time.

Overall, the East Moriches ambulance company was top notch for a small unit that it was. We did have at least one or two paramedics; I believe a couple of EMT-I's and most of its 29 members were very experienced EMT's. All of them were very kind people who were caring. Even though, right away I did not have my certification as an EMT, I was already experienced in dealing with medical emergencies and knew what to do anyway. The certification in the case of some individuals was simply a formality.

All though at the time we were all a bit back woods compared to the Western Suffolk County fire districts; we could hold our own in any situation. We also were quick to arrive on scenes of 911 calls, often beating the Suffolk County police cars to the scene. The member certifications were always current, and we were always on par.

The East Moriches Community Ambulance had a length of highway on Rt. 27 or what is also called Sunrise Highway, in its district. I would say that we were the bad car accident experts. We seemed to get a lot of those calls. When we did, they often required a heavy rescue from the fire department. We also had a small airport in our district. From time to time, we would get 911 calls due to a small plane crash or traumatic injuries from the parachute school that was on the airport. Our members of the ambulance company were experienced in plane crash and airport accidents also. We were a little more experienced than other districts regarding small plane crashes because many other districts didn't airports in their districts.

From Jan 1st, 1995, to December 31st, 1995 I responded to approximately 76 ambulance 911 calls. Responding to the 911 calls was easier and safer then when I was a firefighter.

You just threw on our blue ambulance first responder jacket, put on your latex gloves, jumped on the ambulance you were on your way.

Not so much the glory of the fire truck, but it had its rewarding moments too. Depending on the 911 call, you would get to a scene, stabilize the patient for transport, drive them to the hospital and get them in the emergency room. It took up a lot of time. Each call from start to return would suck up at least 2 hours of your time. Then sometimes you may get a call while you were on the way back from dropping a patient off at the hospital. We were obligated to go directly to that next 911 call. Now you were looking at 4 hours of your time gone. That was all volunteering your time. The same rule was in effect for the fire departments also.

In 1996, I was still an active member of the ambulance. After obtaining my EMT-D certification there seemed to be a low regarding the calls at East Moriches ambulance. I do not remember responding to many calls for the first couple of weeks after obtaining my EMT-D certification.

What interested me at that time was that I could now sign out the first responder ambulance car. All EMT's could do this. I got to keep the car home with me all day and if we had a 911 call, I went right to the scene alone. It was all very exciting and rewarding. Would you believe, every time I signed the thing out, we would hardly get a call from 911 to respond. There were a few 911 calls that I responded to in the first responder unit.

Chapter 800

INCIDENT IN SOUTHAMPTON, NEW YORK

In June of 1996, after only a week or two after obtaining my EMT-D certification, I was hungry and looking to get on any emergency call that I could to prove my worth. I wanted to practice my EMT skills and help the injured or even save a life. I felt it was my duty to save lives.

While driving on a highway in Southampton, New York, I noticed trouble on the road ahead. A truck had been traveling straight. It hit a car crossing in front of it. There was a car driven by a 59-year-old thin woman.

The car was impacted on the driver's side. The woman took the blunt of the impact. There was a police car on the scene that was directing traffic around the disabled car. I saw her still inside the car and not moving. I jerked my car off the road and got out. I opened my trunk, which contained my medical bag with equipment.

I grabbed the bag, as my trunk stayed open. I ran to the car with my heart beating fast. The police officer looked over to me and yelled: "I think she's gone". I said to myself: "I'm not going to let that happen"! I got to her as fast as possible. I could not make entry on the driver's side of the car because the door was crushed.

I then ran to the passenger side opened the door and observed her in a motionless state. She had a non-inflated non-rebreather oxygen mask on her with an oxygen bottle lying by her side as she sat behind the steering wheel unconscious.

The reservoir bag to the mask was not inflated, therefore it was doing little for her. police officers at that time had only limited first aid training. They had started making all police officers, EMT certified until later. Even if they were certified, they kind of stayed away from taking a primary role in a medical emergency. On the other hand, some police officers did a lot of medical care prior to the arrival of the ambulance. This police officer at the scene was an older officer who may not have had the EMT certification. I think what may have happened in this case, was that he started to assess this patient and then applied the oxygen. He probably inflated the reservoir bag on the non-rebreather, but it may have not stay inflated if she did not sustain her breathing.

I noticed that her eyes were slightly open and staring off over the dashboard. There was no sign of life in her gaze.

I looked, listened, and felt for vital signs. That is what EMT's do when assessing an unconscious patient. She was a little pale at first, which also concern me.

I made sure that she had a clear airway and then observed her for signs of respirations as I was feeling for a heartbeat. Her heart was beating fast. Maybe 100 times per minute as to the normal 70 per minute. Then I thought: "Is that her heart or mine?" I got so focused that I tunneled in on my own heartbeat and felt my own heart beating in my fingers. I used my stethoscope just to make sure. I observed that her heart was beating. I then noticed that she wasn't breathing. She had no rise in her chest and no expansion of her lungs. She must have just stopped breathing as I ran up to her. The police officer was over directing traffic and not paying attention to what I had, so I was alone.

I reached for a bag value mask and began giving her air.

This is called rescue breathing. I could not get good air exchange while she was sitting limp in her car. I had to act fast. I knew if I could not get oxygen into her lungs fast, she would die.

I made the quick decision to get her out of the car and on her back by myself. This was so I could maintain a good airway to deliver oxygen to her lungs. I obtained good air exchange with her now that she was out of the car. I provided rescue breathing for about a minute.

Then a young lady who looked only a few years older than me showed up. She identified herself as a doctor and she began checking for a heart rate. She had determined that the victim had no heart rate at that time and began giving chest compressions to the victim.

The initial attempts at the two of us doing CPR together needed synchronization. We did rather well, and we were giving the victim good air flow with good chest compressions.
The local ambulance arrived on the scene. I thought to myself; "Oh good, they got a paramedic with them!" "We are going to save her," as they ran over. They asked if I was good and I said: "Yah, I got it". They left me at my position at the patient's head while giving her respirations with the bag valve mask.

The doctor gave up her position as it is much more exhausting to perform compressions. I believe the paramedic did inject some drugs to attempt to restart the heart.

I can't remember that for sure. The victim was turning grey when the defibrillator was affixed to her. Her heart displayed a shock worthy heart rhythm on the defibrillator monitor. The paramedic that arrived with the ambulance yelled that he would be using the defibrillator on the victim. He yelled: "All clear!"

We broke contact with the victim as the paramedic delivered the shock. The victim twitched from the electricity, but we had no luck. We continued CPR. After another few cycles of CPR, the paramedic repeated the shock again and I think a third time with no success. It was hot and exhaustion fell among all of us.

We had tried to resuscitate her for probably what totaled about 10 minutes in all. The decision had to be made on what to do next. The doctor had made the declaration there at the scene and the woman was pronounced dead. We certainly gave it a heck of a shot and wondered why we could not bring her back. I gently helped the victim into her black body bag. I still felt that I should protect her. I gently placed her to rest in the ambulance for transport. I then zipped her up in her body bag. I touched her head and told her "I'm sorry".

A few days later, I had heard that we had not been able to save her because her neck was severed in the back. I was very disappointed to hear that. I never noticed it when I was with her that day.

By July 17th, 1996, that same summer would turn into a sad summer. For some, that sad year of 1996, turned into a sad lifetime. If I only knew what was to come ahead.

Chapter 9

JULY 15TH 1996
SOUTHAMPTON, NEW YORK

On July 15th, 1996, my son was born in Southampton hospital. I was present for the delivery and medically vigilant of everything during the birth. It was smooth and uneventful. For the next few days, I was visiting him in the hospital while still working at the 106th Rescue Wing and responding to 911 calls with the East Moriches ambulance.

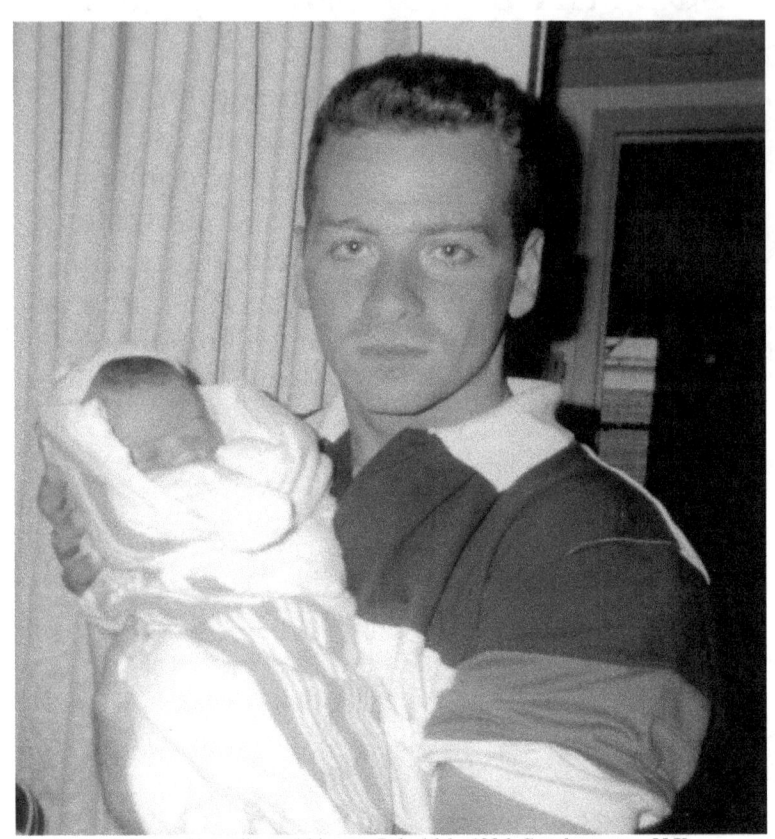
*Barry Donadio and his son July 16th, 1996, Southampton, N.Y.
The day before the TWA Flight 800 crash*

The following is the account of my observations on the evening of July 17th, 1996. I felt that this night was different than any other typical night or typical ambulance call. This account was originally meant to be observed only by my family. I had not touched it since July 21st, 2005. That is when I placed my TWA Flt 800 Witness Account with other documents and accounts that I keep in a file. I designed this file for my family to open upon my death. It has instructions, insurance papers, religious documents, confidential personal writings, photos, videos, and my entire family history.

I have redacted some information for multiple reasons. Sometimes for protecting the victim's identity, the first responder's identity and other reasons.

I will not offer any reason, opinion, or conclusion as to why TWA flight 800 crashed. I will describe what I observed and what I was thinking on July 17th, 1996.

I am on the side or the people and the government of the United States equally. I have taken equal oath to serve them both equally. My allegiance always has been and always will be to the United States of America.

Chapter 10

WHAT THE HELL

On the night of July 17th, 1996, I was driving westbound on Montauk Highway. I was in East Moriches almost at the border east and Center Moriches, New York. At about 8:30pm, I observed two Suffolk County police cars and one Suffolk County police military type humvee vehicle. They were driving East on Montauk Highway. They all had their red and white emergency top lights on and sirens on.

I encountered them while engaged in a dark part of East Moriches on a bend in the road. I was probably going about 55 mph and the Police vehicles that came out of nowhere were driving at a very high rate of speed, approximately (redacted).

The first police cars that approached had nearly collided with me. I think we missed each other by only inches. I am sure my car surprised them also. There was no one on the road that night and the near collision almost killed me and one of the police officers. I knew that the humvee with police markings was assigned to the Suffolk police marine bureau. You hardly ever saw that thing respond to anything. It was new and more of a show piece than anything else. I had never seen the Suffolk County Police (Redacted).. Since I too was a police officer, I figured they were responding to a police officer that had been shot or something of a similar serious nature.

Chapter 11

SIGNAL 27

I wondered why the East Moriches Community Ambulance units did not get notified about, what I thought was a call for a police officer injured.

I checked my ambulance pager and the volume had accidently been turned all the way down. I turned it up halfway through a transmitting communication. It was the Suffolk County medical communications (MEDCOM). I heard the call for East Moriches ambulance to respond to the East Moriches Coast Guard station for a signal 27.

"Signal 27?" I said to myself. This was the code for need to respond to a call for a plane crash.

It was one of those codes that every firefighter and EMT knew of, but rarely used until that day. When it was used prior in relation to our ambulance, it was for a small place. I never expected it to be an aircraft the size of a 747.

That code has not been used on such a grand scale since the Avianca Flight 52 plane crash on Long Island in 1990. I simply didn't know what we had waiting for us. Was it a small little 4 seat plane or was this the big one? MEDCOM didn't say during their radio transmission. Judging by the behavior of the responding police officers, it is probably the big one. I abruptly pulled over, did a u turn and floored the gas pedal. I headed east towards where the police cars were going and in the direction of the East Moriches Community Ambulance garage that was on Pine Ave. I was only moments from the ambulance garage and coming in fast.

Chapter 12

RESPONSE OF EAST MORICHES AMBULANCE

I made it to the East Moriches Community Ambulance garage in a maximum of three minutes from when I first observed the responding police cars. At the time I had arrived at the garage, both East Moriches ambulances and the first responder truck were gone. I could not believe that both ambulances were already driving to the scene. I could not see how that was possible. They all must have been there before the call went over the radio and simply jumped in the ambulances and were on their way. In my opinion the East Moriches ambulance company responded with speed and professionalism. They had to have arrived at the Coast Guard station in only 2 minutes or so.

I was standing in shock at the ambulance garage looking at two open and empty ambulance bays. I was about to drive to the call in my car. Then a car pulled up, fast. It was (Redacted).

He was a paramedic with our ambulance and a dam good person to have for this call. He saw that we missed the ambulances, so he said, "Get in!" I got in his car we put on the green emergency dashboard EMT emergency light. We then raced off to the Coast Guard station. It was the designated staging area for first responders and emergency apparatus to respond to. Responding police, ambulances and fire trucks responded there.

Chapter 13

GEE THAT'S STRANGE

By this time, which could not have totaled more the ten minutes from when I first heard the call transmitted on the radio, the Suffolk County Police had the entire area on lock down. We had to show our ambulance identification cards prior to even getting to the Coast Guard station.

This was an order to pass through blocked roads that they posted. Prior to this evening, I had responded to 6 years of 911 calls in the capacity of a firefighter, EMT and military police officer. I never was required to show my identification when responding to a call for service.

That evening, if you were a member of a different ambulance district that was not specifically called to the scene by MEDCOM, you were not permitted to pass through the police roadblocks.

This was quite bizarre. Normally you wanted to have as many EMT's there as possible. EMT's were always glad to have other EMT's on a scene with them. The more EMT's the better. Especially for a plane crash with mass casualties. At big incidents, it was not important what district an EMT served, only that they were an EMT and helping victims. This night was different.

The Suffolk police were in a different mode. They seemed to act like a military force that was unknown to us and not the usual police that we worked with daily.

The police seemed to become even more vigilant later as they kept the number of responders to the Coast Guard station to the lowest amount of people possible.

Some departments were even sent back to their respective firehouses later in the evening.

This quite opposite of what medical people want.

We wanted manpower and assistance, not responders being sent away. These instances of law enforcement behavior and extraordinary vigilance of the police were the first odd clues that lead to a much odder evening.

Chapter 14

FIRST RESPONDERS AT THE TWA FLIGHT 800 CRASH

Upon my first arrival inside the Coast Guard station, I observed approximately 20 Suffolk County police cars that had responded and parked within the Coast Guard station perimeter. There were about 15 ambulances that included both East Moriches ambulances.

The other ambulances were from our adjoining districts. They were most likely called out automatically when the 911 call came into MEDCOM. All those ambulances were staged inside the Coast Guard station perimeter. I believe there was a total of about 3 class A fire trucks there as well. The police officers that I encountered inside the Coast Guard station behaved like the police we were used to. They acted friendly and gentlemanly.

They did not display the same vigilance that the police officers outside the gates displayed. Everyone there deserved thanks for their response that evening. The night would be long.

Chapter 15

SURVIVORS

As a new emergency medical technician at this call, I was a preparing for what I may soon encounter. The East Moriches Community Ambulance vice president (A name redacted) was on the scene. He was a great leader and very kind. He briefed me on what he knew. He told me that we expected survivors to start arriving at our location in about 45 minutes or so. The reports were, that the ones that were alive, were critical. This was somewhat comforting news to me.

At least there would be some that we could save. I suddenly became very confident, ready, and ready to help the survivors.

After that, all the medical personnel at the Coast Guard station began to set up a triage area. The original location for the triage area was going to be in a garage type building on the North side of the main building.

It had a boat ramp. So many things went through my mind in preparation for the survivors. I began to recite medical remedies for traumatic injuries in my mind. I was ready to assist my first TWA Flight 800 patient, when they would arrive.

I was thinking that I wanted to provide the best care for the arriving survivors and save them. The images of what I may soon see, flooded my imagination. I guess you would call it, mental preparation for the worst. I somewhat tormented myself by these thoughts in a kind of over preparation.

I had to take a moment to make an important decision. I could either fear what I was about to see and be useless to the survivors or be strong and professional. I decided to be strong for my country and my people. I wanted to tend to the worst injured survivor that I could find. I would never get my chance.

A low in the action occurred and there was some waiting and sitting around. Everything was set up and ready. Some good time went by with no other information passed on to us. Then, even more time went by. We were then past the original 45 minutes that survivors were supposed to arrive. We waited and waited. Then we heard that we had time to drive quickly to the gas station and buy some snacks and water for our ambulance crew. I volunteered to drive quick in our marked orange colored first responder truck.

Remember, this was a marked unit and it had red and white emergency lights on its roof. We drove to the gas station on the Southeast corner of Montauk Highway and Pine Street. We bought a bunch of things and headed back to the Coast Guard station fast.

We maintained radio communication with our ambulance crews at the Coast Guard station just in case they needed us back faster.

While driving back to the Coast Guard station, I had noticed that the Suffolk County police had a police officer on every corner.

This was from the intersection of Pine Ave. and Montauk Highway, all the way to the Coast Guard Station. Even though the police just observed us leave the Coast Guard station, they checked our identification at every corner on the way back inside. This was unheard of at the time. "They're checking our ID in a marked ambulance vehicle?" I said. "Gee, that's strange."

We arrived back at the Coast Guard station with our snacks and drinks. We had heard that the cops arrested some reporter who tried to penetrate their roadblocks. We knew they weren't taking any nonsense that evening.

As for the survivors, we were still waiting for them. Remember that on that evening, we had no idea that we would eventually have not one survivor.

We believed in what we were told, and we were waiting patiently. There was some prayer by me during that wait as others did what they needed to do to prepare themselves.

The reality of all lives lost would be the worst trick played on us that night. The inadvertent misinformation spread that night, made this tragedy worse for us. It was the same as telling a little child that there was no Santa Claus. It was that same disappointment. That loss of hope and the creation of despair is what hurt us first responders most.

Two hours went past with no arriving bodies or survivors. I began to question if we would ever see a survivor. It was an unofficial and unspoken vibe that we would not see a survivor. We all knew the reality, yet nothing had been announced. We still had that small light of hope in our hearts, but that light was to be extinguished fast.

Chapter 16

THE FIRST BOATS ARRIVE

The word came. We had received notice that a boat was coming into the Coast Guard station. I walked quickly to the North dock of the Coast Guard station to observe.

(Redacted). So many boats came that evening, (Redacted). I would say it were a Coast Guard boat that was the first one to arrive. The East Moriches ambulance crews and a team of the Suffolk County police emergency services unit (ESU), all took up a position of observation on the North dock. We all watched the slow approaching boat (Redacted). I saw no survivors.

The horror began as we stared in a shallow gaze. The sights that made every experienced police officer, firefighter and EMT lose composer.

For a moment we were all like little children, frightened of the dark. Scared and hopeless, our mouths involuntarily opened as we watched. The images began to deliver a slow and lasting shock. I looked at the other first responders that were on the dock with me.

I saw how we all looked, and I immediately adjusted my demeanor. I stiffened upper my lips, opened my eyes wide and provided a blank, serious look to anyone observing me. This is a look that I still have to this day, and it can be observed in pictures of me today. My colleges continued their gaze as the bodies became more and more visible.

Chapter 17

THE AGONY

The deceased passengers of TWA flight 800 were piled up on the decks of the boats that brought them to us. The boats were sometimes small and filled to the rafters. This sounds like unwarranted and cruel treatment of the victims. I bear witness, that there was no other way to bring them home. A silence came over the Coast Guard station as that first boat pulled in and floated up next to the dock.

Everything was in my full view. I remember the faces of those who died. All this will always remain in my memory forever.

Chapter 18

DISEMBARKING

There were two very young coast guardsmen that were there. They were there waiting where the boats would pull in. The coast guardsmen looked so young to me. They could have only been 18 years old or so.

These two brave American heroes unloaded mostly every corpse that I observed that night. The horrors that those two men experienced, is unthinkable. I don't think when they signed up for the Coast Guard, they thought they would be unloading bodies.

Our ambulance crew still observing, as the two coast guardsmen did their duty. One man at the head and one at the legs of each victim. They would struggle off the boat and on to the wood dock.

I observed many different traumatic injuries that the victims suffered. As the bodies were brought from the boat to the dock, blood would drip and splatter. I didn't understand why the blood didn't all come out while the victims were in the water.

The bodies were laid on the dock from the decks of the boats that brought them in.

When the bodies were laid on the dock, they sometimes hit the dock hard. Each body made a sound when it hit the dock.

You can mimic this sound by making a fist and hitting a wood table. It makes a thump sound. These sounds disturbed me a great deal. I was going to protest what was happening for the sake of the victims. I wanted better treatment of the bodies, but there was no other way to unload them.

I then remembered that I was only a volunteer that evening and nothing more. It was upsetting to see. I gathered myself and began to rationalize this.

There was little time, and more boats were coming. There was also very limited access to the dock where we were. I think we were allowed on the dock because it was our ambulance district. I think the ambulance crews from other districts were in the perimeter of the station but may not have observed the bodies that we did.

I promise that every victim I encountered received my prayers. I could no longer be utilized as an EMT that evening because there were no survivors coming back. I was a vigilant observer and a mechanism of prayer for those who suffered. When I observed another victim, I prayed for them. Then another one came in; they got a prayer too. It was the very least I could do for them. I remained in service to the victims and always will be as I keep the in my prayers.

Chapter 19

HORROR

One man that I remember, had been cut completely in half at the waist. His face had a look on it like he had a happy expression. His face appeared to have a smile. His eyes were open and looking at me.

His face was stuck in that position. He was about 55 years old, 250 pounds. I think he was tall. Maybe six feet tall. He was bald with some hair on the sides of his head.

I later reviewed photos of the TWA passengers and this man appeared to be: (TWA Flt. 800 victim's identity redacted)

I remember a headless body that evening. It was lifted out of the boat that had been brought it to the dock. It had some of the internal portions of head and spinal column still intact where the head would have been. It was bloody with bone exposed. It was troubling to see because it was a body with a bloody stump as a head. It was eye catching and horrific. I began to pray for that poor soul too.

I remember a young girl being unloaded from the boat. She seemed to be only about 12 years old, but she could have been older. She was more gently treated than the other bodies. My eyes watered as her eyes were open and lifeless. I gazed on to her limp body and I was searching for life and could not find any in her from where I was standing.

She was so beautiful, and I assume she was one of the (people or person on TWA Flight 800 redacted). Her body was intact, and she maintained her clothing.

A passenger that I remember very well was a female between 25 to 30 years old. She had black frizzy hair. She was very thin, and she had on black clothing. She was wearing a dress or a skirt. She was laying in one of the boats that brought her in.

She had caught my eye as she was being taken off the boat. She was at the front of the boat that brought her in. When then lifted her up, her face was facing me. Her head lifted before her legs. Her head was up off the boat about 2 feet.

I said to myself "My God". I saw that her face was dripping off her. I didn't understand what I was seeing. I didn't notice any other injuries to her body. I only observed the right side of her face dropping one foot off her head. It caused one to stare. I had asked (Redacted) how that could happen. I was told that she must have floated in the water and exposed to the jet fuel. The fuel breaks down and degrades the skin. This caused it to do what it did on the woman's face. Her skin stretched and acted like melting caramel.

Later, I reviewed pictures of the TWA victims, and I am certain that it was (TWA Flt 800 victim's identity redacted).

Chapter 20

MAYBE WE CAN SAVE ONE

Many of the bodies were completely intact that evening and this shocked me. I was thinking we can try to save one. Many of them looked like they may have died from drowning. They very well may have had fatal broken necks or even every bone in their bodies broken. By only observing them, they seemed that they may have simply drowned. I said myself " Did we let the drowned? We couldn't save one?" Many showed no obvious signs of any trauma at all, and some maintained their outer clothing.

I thought to myself, we can try CPR. It could be possible to try it. Only maybe, but it could happen. Maybe we can save one. This may have been only a potluck shot. I was willing to give it a try, but there was no opportunity. The bodies brought in by the boats were already written off as lost.

They had been most likely in the water up two hours already. Then, add the time it took the boats to arrive to us would have added at least another hour before I saw any of them. I remember wondering if there were originally survivors, perhaps they may have ended up drowning. This was the reason for us being originally told of survivors. I also thought to myself that the force and speed of the 747 finally hitting the water would have ended the life of all passengers. The trauma of hitting the water at 200 plus mile per hour, would most certainly end their lives. I always leave room for miracles. We may never know the entire truth of what happened to the plane until others step forward and share their experience such as I have. More evidence may surface that can also offer a different perspective as to what may or may not have happened.

Chapter 21

THE TRAMA INFLICTED ON THE PASSENGERS TWA FLT 800

Most of the victims that I had witnessed that evening had no clothes on. They had no shoes, socks, pants, or shirts. Unless I have described otherwise on certain victims, the men maintained only their boxer shorts or underwear. The women maintained their bras and underwear. I knew that night, the force of the plane hitting the water did this. But I asked myself, how did some of the others still maintain their outer garments? How and why were some of the passengers completely torn apart or cut in half and others only looked like they drowned and maintained their clothing? I thought that this could only mean one thing.

The passengers with their clothes still on, did not fall victim to the same trauma as the others. How? This was all in my mind that evening as I began to question what did in fact happen.

'

Another point is (10 words redacted) that evening. (7 words redacted) torso which resembled a body. They were either cut in half, without arms, legs, or heads. The other victims that I observed were only masses that made up body parts. The parts were recovered in the water that evening.

An arm, a leg or just maybe a head would be all mixed together and placed into a bag. I can describe these bags as huge potato sacks. They were not potato sacks but seem very similar in material and color. Each bag seemed to be about 150 pounds. That weight was all body parts mixed in together. I observed at least 15 of these bags. The bags were placed on the dock when the boats brought them in. They made the same noise as the bodies did when they hit the dock.

Chapter 22

BURNED?

None of the bodies or body parts that I had observed that evening was burned. None showed any sign of being exposed to intense heat. No black charring on their skin. No heat blisters, nothing. All of them looked like they had died of massive trauma and or drowning. I remember after that night the news reporting that the victims we burned, and I questioned this. I knew right away that this was not accurate. I spoke to many first responders after that evening. They all stated that they never observed any bodies that showed any sign of burns. It is possible that there may have been bodies that were burned, I just never had contact with them.

Chapter 23

RYDER TRUCKS?

During that evening, I noticed that two or three Ryder rental trucks were at the scene. I could not understand how they would have arrived at the Coast Guard station so quickly. I noticed that they were refrigerated. I speculated that they must have been trucks from a coroner's office. Maybe from New York City. I am almost certain the bodies went into these trucks and were transported off the Coast Guard station. This was under the cloak of Ryder company. The arrival of these trucks was about the same time that the first boats carrying bodies arrived at the Coast Guard station. A few weeks later, my curiosity got to me. I began to inquire about these trucks. I called the Ryder company and asked if they had any refrigerated trucks I could rent. They stated that they don't have any in their fleet.

Chapter 24

INSIDE THE EAST MORICHES COAST GUARD STATION

While some of the bodies were being unloaded, I needed to use the bathroom. There were tables set up in the bays of the Coast Guard station. These were the bays that would normally house the small boats that were stationed there. They had a ramp leading up to the bays. The doors were open so anyone who was at the station that night could walk right in. The table were set up like a triage. It was a triage for bodies. There were people who resembled doctors or corners (I don't know who they were) that were examining the bodies on the tables. The bodies were being examined in full view of all in the open bay.

When I walked in the open bay to access the bathroom, I did not know this was going on. I walked right into an examination taking place.

The examiner had tweezers and was picking through what I could only describe as a stump with boxer shorts and legs.

These were the remains of a very pale colored Caucasian male, with black hairy legs. The sight of it, caught me off guard.

I was not paying attention and looking the other direction when I looked down and saw the stump with legs. I thought to myself that this was an unfortunate person now reduced to a stump. I kept my mouth shut, maintained my professional composure, and walked on to use the rest room.

I remember the restroom being upstairs in the Coast Guard station. There were (Redacted)

Officials in what appeared to be secret meetings with closed doors on the second floor. I observed Coast Guard officers coming out of these meetings. There were others in these meetings also (Redacted). I remember a U.S. Marine Officer that was at the Coast Guard station that evening. I believe he was present before the bodies began to come in at the Coast Guard Station. The Marine was wearing his dress blue and tan uniform. He was a Caucasian, approximately 6'2, about 45 years old, shaved blonde hair. He was very slim, and he looked like he knew what he was doing that night. I believe he was a Lieutenant Colonel, and he was the only U.S. Marine that I observed at the Coast Guard station that evening. He also seemed very confident with everything going on. He had what appeared to be the highest level of control and confidence compared to everyone else there.

When I first noticed him, I could not understand why the Marines were there at the Coast Guard station for this incident. He looked as if he was calling the shots of what was being done that night regarding some of the issues. Coast Guard officers were seen consulting in him. I think he was one of the highest-ranking military officers on the scene. I watched him much of the night because it all seemed very intriguing to me.

Chapter 25

WHO'S IN CHARGE HERE?

During the night some of the odd things and the out of place officials, began to overwhelm my curiosity. There seemed to be two or three different agendas at the Coast Guard station during the first hours of the tragedy. It seemed that there was a disconnect regarding who was the head agency, who was giving the orders and what they were. The agendas were advanced by (3 entities redacted) I knew that it was not my place to ask, but I did anyway. I went up to a Coast Guard officer and asked, "Who's in charge here?" The officer pointed over to the dock where the bodies were being unloaded and said, "That guy". I looked over to him and I noticed that I had been watching that guy a lot also. I was watching him prior to my question. He was or was identified as an Army doctor. He was wearing a U.S. Army camouflage battle dress uniform. I remember that he was wearing the rank of Colonel.

He had black hair, 6 feet tall, estimated 220 pounds, he must have been in his early 50's. I observed him directing all the operations regarding the bodies. He was there on the dock directing some of the young Coast Guardsmen for the whole night.

He was feverishly concern for the young Coast Guardsmen who were exposed to unloading the bodies from the boats. Blood from the bodies mixed with the sea water as many of the bodies were a mix between being waterlogged or blood logged. He would take a hose and spray the dock down after each load of bodies were taken away of the dock. It was hard to hear him, but he was directing the others on the dock and looked like he was in charge. My question of who was in charge was not really meant to identify an individual. I asked the question because I wanted to know what entity was in charge.

My question was not answered properly until I asked the (An entity redacted) that were at the Coast Guard station that evening. They insisted that the military oversaw the entire operation because (A reason redacted). I thought to myself; "The military?"

There were a few FBI agents present at the Coast Guard station, or at least, they presented themselves as such. They wore civilian clothing. They let us do our job and there seemed to be a good working relationship between them and the first responders, early onset. It was good to have them there and they did their part in the efforts that evening.

There were also two men from (An entity redacted), They were permitted unrestricted access to the bodies. I knew one of these men personally. He was there in good intent.

Chapter 26

IMPERSONATOR

During the evening I observed at least 3 different helicopters had landed in the small space of the Coast Guard station. The landing zone was tight, and I don't think it was an easy landing for the pilots. The helicopters had no problem landing since they were guided in the landing zone by ground guide. This ground guide was in fact, an impersonator.

He must have arrived very early in the evening or may have already been on the grounds prior to the plane crash. He was wearing a green U.S. Army flight suit. He was a tall black man with a Jamaican accent. I noticed him immediately, because seemed to not fit in and was strange in his demeanor. I can say that he did a dam good job guiding in helicopters when they were landing at the Coast Guard station.
I believe he was wearing the rank of Lt. Colonel. It was interesting that many high-ranking officials were in the helicopters that were guided in by this crafty fellow. Of course, everyone else was busy and didn't really notice him for most of the night. I began to watch this man and dissect his behavior.

I noticed that he was wearing a different unit patch on each arm of his uniform. This indicates that he was in combat while serving the unit that was indicated on his right shoulder. He didn't seem to carry himself like other combat veterans I have known before that evening.

Those veterans have a certain way about them. With great curiosity, I approached him. I had to remember that I had no authority to do anything. I could only act as a police officer when I was on duty at the 106th Rescue Wing Security Police section on the Gabreski Airbase.
I asked him about his patch on his right shoulder. It was the patch of the (Army unit redacted) division. He seemed confused and nervous by my question. It became obvious to me that he was not telling the truth. I broke contact with him and immediately reported his behavior to a police officer at the Coast Guard station. I am not sure if the officer that I explained this to, took the matter very serious. I know he did not go right over to the impersonator and check his identification. I know that the police officer kept him under observation after I reported it. I do not know if the impersonator was discovered that evening or later. It was not until the next day or so, that his actions were reported in the local papers.

Chapter 27

MYSTERIOUS PHOTOGRAPHER

There was a man in civilian clothing wearing a white shirt at the Coast Guard station. He seemed to arrive about the same time the first boat of bodies arrived. He was a short, Asian man who looked like he was in his early thirties. He was a real professional at photography. He had a very expensive camera, and he wore a bandoleer of film. I guessed he had at least 50 rolls of film on him. He took pictures of everything, without restriction. He did not even yield to taking pictures of all the bodies. He took a picture on a average of once every 15 seconds or so. He did this the entire time I was on the North dock. I do not recall him ever pointing his camera directly at me, but he probably got me in the background of some pictures that he took.

He seemed to get a photo of everything and every person there on that evening. If not directly taking a picture of the target, he would include you in the background. It was certainly a documentary. He kind of made me feel like he was casually trying to get everyone present on film also. He always seemed to get as many people as he could in a photo even if he was taking a picture of something else. He must have taken 1000 photos that evening. I am sure he took even more than that. He had unrestricted access to everything. Earlier, the photographer was challenged by a young Coast Guard officer. I overheard the officer question a more senior Coast Guard officer regarding the photographer. The senior Officer said, "He's ok, He's with (An entity redacted)". The photographer continued with his work uninterrupted and never again questioned.

The bodies continued to come, and he continued his gloomy work. It seemed that he was very experienced in documenting bodies and incidents like this.

The photographer showed no signs of the event affecting him whatsoever. I wondered who would get to review the pictures and how I was going to try to get copies of them for documentary purposes. I realized that it would probably be an impossibility.

Chapter 28

THE EVENING COMES TO AN END

Most of the long evening, I remained on the dock. I was in full view of all the bodies being unloaded from the armada of boats that came in carrying them. My East Moriches Community Ambulance coworkers were there with me. A few members of the Suffolk County Police ESU were also still there with us. I estimate that it was about 4am on July 18th, 1996, when we were told to vacate. The FBI special agent in charge gave the order, which was given to the vice president of the East Moriches Community Ambulance. He gave me the order.

The order was to limit the number of persons on the dock area. So, instead of about 6 ambulance personnel on the dock, there would now be only 2. The police ESU were allowed to remain.
We were still permitted to remain on the grounds of the Coast Guard station. We just had to remain with our ambulance where it was parked in the compound. There really was not much more to see at that point. From 4am on, there seemed to be a big push for limiting the amount of people in observance of the bodies.

At 5am, the vice president of our ambulance came and asked us if we wanted to leave for the night. East Moriches would only keep one ambulance crew on the scene which consisted of a total of 4 people. A few of us departed the Coast Guard station. We arrived back to the ambulance garage. We put the ambulance back into operational condition. I went home, went to sleep, and continued with my life the next day. I was so tiered I don't think I signed the ambulance call logbook to get credit for the work I did that night.

Chapter 29

SALVAGE OPERATIONS

The East Moriches Community Ambulance provided an ambulance to the Coast Guard station, it remained on standby for salvage operations. Divers from the military, fire departments and the police were at the Coast Guard station for weeks. Our ambulance was stationed there in case the salvage persons got hurt. On occasion they did get hurt. It was a tremendous undertaking that included 1000's of hours of work. I did volunteer and stay at the Coast Guard station in the days after the crash. I think maybe twice. I do not remember if I did more than that. One of those times a police officer from New York City police (NYPD) got hurt during a salvage operation. He was fine and I don't even think we took him to the hospital. Other East Moriches ambulance members did volunteer for weeks after the crash to standby at the Coast Guard station.

Chapter 30

GABRESKI
AIR NATIONAL GUARD BASE

The 106th rescue wing was involved in the rescue and salvage of TWA Flight 800. Some people later blamed the 106th Rescue Wing for the downing of TWA Flight 800.

About a day or two after the crash, I was back at the base working my full-time job as a security police officer on the base. The 106th Rescue Wing consisted mostly of good old Long Island men and women that were devoted to their country and their people. I was surprised and a bit proud to find out that the recovered parts to TWA Flight 800 were being stored on our base. Having a part in protecting the parts gave me a sense of pride because I felt like I was still helping the victims in some way. The parts were being laid out in one of the large airplane hangars on our base.

When I first heard that the parts were on the base, I drove right over to check it out. I had full access to the parts of the plane. There was no restriction to me. I did not touch any of the parts, so I don't think the agents that were there in civilian clothes considered me a threat. I am not sure if I went to work at the base on July 18th or July 19th.

All the parts I observed were small and too heavy to float. They were not recovered quickly, because they were not floating on the water surface. These parts would have required a diver to recover them from the bottom of the sea floor.

All the parts that I observed were small metallic in composer and too heavy to float. I thought to myself " How did they get those parts here so fast when recovery of the bodies was priority?"

How did these parts come to us in the hanger in one or two days? I know that the divers were recovering bodies, not parts. From my understanding, not that early. So, I could only assume that maybe those parts may have been removed from the bodies when the bodies were recovered. It is possible that some of those parts impaled in some of the victims. When a body was recovered, it may have had a part of the plane with it.

That was the only explanation I could think of at the time. Before a month past, it was decided that the hanger would be too small to store all the parts and the TWA Flight 800 pieces and parts were moved to a hangar in Calverton, New York.

Chapter 31

THE MASS CONFUSION AT THE STROKE OF NINE

Many know that on July 17th, 1996, there was not really any question of what caused the crash of TWA Flight 800. It was not until a short period of time after the tragedy, that confusion began to stir about what happened to the plane. So, the theories and the blame of what happened to TWA Flight 800 became the focus of an entire nation and the world. Some people made a career of trying to uncover evidence of a cover up. Informed people may know more. Let's always remember the victims of this tragedy. Eventually, all your questions and concerns will be answered.

Continue searching for answers. In time, you will know everything you seek to know. Always follow your heart and it will lead you to the truth you seek.

Labeling people and shifting blame will not lead you to where you will find answers. Immoral attacks and destroying good people are not in line with God's work. Expose alleged facts and do it carefully, without hurting any persons or entities.

(Additional redactions)

Chapter 32

AIR SHOW TRADGEDY IN WESTHAMPTON

On June 22, 1997, there was an air show at the Gabreski Air National Guard base. I was assigned to work the flight line area of the base and provide security and law enforcement for the event. I worked that day in the capacity of a security police officer. I was armed with a Berretta 92F 9mm pistol. I patrolled in a marked Air Force police pickup truck. It was the best truck in our fleet at that time. It was a new and big Ford F-350. It had four doors and was designated as security police patrol truck # 842. It was fast for its time.

There were approximately 15,000 spectators at the air show. It was a hot summer day on Long Island. It was exciting to see all the planes on display. I had never been to an air show prior to that day.

At 1:50pm, I began patrolling the flight line area of the base. I parked the police truck near the hangar closest to the base fire house. I engaged in conversation with a spectator who was a WWII veteran. He was telling me about the war, and I was really enjoying the conversation. He had his old identification cards from the war.

I had his wallet in my hand and was looking at his old military identification, when suddenly I heard yelling. I looked up and observed a civilian. He pointed out near the southern part of the airport runway.

I gazed out and saw a wreckage on fire. I did not see what happened and only assumed it was a plane crash. I had tunnel vision as I ran to my police truck. I never gave the old man his wallet. I still had it in my hand.

His wallet was with me in the truck as I responded to the crash site. I never realized I had it. That's how focused I was on getting to the crash. I jumped into police truck and turned on the red and white emergency lights. I cranked the siren on to yelp mode and I was throttle up on the gas pedal. I could not floor the gas pedal until I got clear of all the spectators on the flight line. The crash site was only about a quarter of a mile away from my position. I still had to get there and save whoever it was in that fiery wreck. All I could see is black smoke rising in a tiny streaming mushroom cloud. It only took seconds for me to clear the hardtop and hit the grass. From there on, I had an unimpeded drive to the wreck. I was alone and I would be on the scene first. No time to plan a rescue. I was just going to get there and pull anyone I saw away from the fire. The police truck hit the grass and I floored that thing! The siren was screaming and emergency lights blaring.

The truck started getting away from my control because I was now off road. I hit a few bumps and hit my head on the roof.

I forgot to put my seat belt on. Nothing hurt, I was amped up anyway. I had to let off the gas to safely arrive to the wreckage. That police truck was extra-long. It didn't handle well going fast for off-road responses. I estimate that it only took me 30 to 40 seconds to get to the wreckage site.

There was an unrecognized hero that beat me to the scene. It was a state highway department worker who must have been watching the air show on the south road of the base. He attacked the flames with a fire extinguisher that he deployed from his highway department truck. As soon as the plane crashed, he began spraying the wreck down with his fire extinguisher.

He gallantly aided and gave valuable seconds to the responding units to further extinguish the fire. His original position was only about 50 yards from the wreck.

I then arrived on scene. For the pilot in the wreck, it must have been an eternity to wait for me to get there. I got there so fast that I had limited options of what I could do to save him. I was alone. No other police officers, no firefighters, and no ambulance. The fire raged on and engulfed the plane with the pilot in the cockpit.

I slammed the brakes to the police truck and stopped just on the edge of the burning grass. The entire 25-yard radius was completely engulfed in flames. I could see the pilot through the smoke and flames. He was somehow still sitting upright in his seat, but there was no plane. It was in pieces around him. It was one of the strangest things I had ever seen. I have no idea how he ended up in that position.

I later reviewed video of the accident and he had nose-dived right into the ground.

From what I could see, the pilot was still alive. He is alive and on fire." At that very second, I remembered the promise that I had made to myself on June 6th, 1990. I promised myself, that I would sacrifice myself to prevent someone burning alive.

I did not want the guilt of failure again. Still alone, with no other first responders on scene, I made my move. Only seconds had passed since I arrived on scene. I had not made much of a plan. I was only going to get to the pilot out. I ran toward him in desperation. I got a about 2 feet, and it was too hot. It was even hotter than the car fire in June 1990. The pilot was on fire, and I wasn't getting to the pilot to aid him.

Everything was on fire and the pilot was right in the middle of it. I could only watch until a firetruck with a water cannon would arrive. The pilot appeared to have worn a fire-retardant suit and a helmet. This gear did not help him in this case because he was on fire.

Only seconds had passed, when the 106th rescue wing fire department arrived. They arrived in that scene and blasted that fire with their water cannon. I was so proud of the firefighter that arrived right behind me. The Water cannon blasted the fire with hundreds of gallons of cool water with foam which quickly put out the flame. They targeted the pilot with the water cannon to protect him from the flames. The 106th rescue wing fire department had two of those huge airport firetrucks that could spray an area and put out tremendous fires in seconds. That is exactly what they did. That first fire truck made a 30 second blast. I was now soaked as I got in cross hairs of the water cannon. They weren't about to slow down if I was in the way. I am sure the firefighter saw me and blasted the fire anyway. It was the correct decision.

The fire was out, and I looked over to the pilot. He began to lean forward. It looked like he was moving in slow motion. His body seemed restricted in movement. Obviously, from what he had been through. I then thought, maybe the fire-retardant suit did provide him protection. He was still alive.

He was still there sitting in his chair and unable to get up or out.

The fire was hot, and the ground was charred. It was still very hot, even with the flames out. The firetrucks were still needed to spray the ground because it was so hot. By that time an ambulance was by my side, and other security police officers arrived. We ran over to the pilot. The emergency medical technician (EMT) from the ambulance did a extremely great job. The professionalism was benchmark. We could not move the pilot. The EMT oversaw the patient (pilot). Care was given to the pilot as fast as humanly possible. The pilot said something we approached him. I could not completely comprehend his words. It sounded like mumbling. I am guessing he said, "Get me out of here!" This is because I heard the EMT reply "we can't move you until we check you out first!" I could not believe the pilot even spoke.

There were now plenty of medical people attending to the pilot and I broke off to maintain protection of the scene.

A security police supervisor arrived on scene, and we began to secure the crash site. It was a crime scene until determined otherwise. At that point, we still didn't even know what happened. At that moment a photographer showed up right there taking photos of the pilots' sufferings. We removed him from there immediately.

We had only been on scene about 2 minutes to this point. It all happened that fast.

The New York State Police joined us on the scene of the accident. I looked over at the pilot as he appeared to sit lifeless in his seat. I thought he was dead, but he wasn't. I observed the ambulance personal taking off the pilot's helmet and flight suit. I felt so sorry for him. His skin was not black from burns, but very red in some areas. The skin was peeling off from the extreme heat. The fire-retardant suit helped him a little. It seemed to repeal the flames but not the intense heat. The pilot's helmet was then removed. This revealed a terrible image.

The pilot's face was battered. I realized the extreme pain he must be feeling. His face was pink and burned. His mouth was burned. This reduced the size of it. His lips were gone. His hair was gone, maybe just a little still left. His right eye came out of the socket and remained on his check. It was still attached by a nerve that went from the back of the eye to the eye socket. I just knew that he would not be able to live. The miracle was that he was still alive. We provided everything that we could to save him so he could somehow continue his life. We all did our part. He suffered a mortal wound, but this did not impede our efforts to save him. As the EMT's were helping him, I was praying while still doing my duties. It was all I could do.

Everything to this point only took a few minutes. I recall that a doctor had arrived on scene. He was originally a spectator at the air show that had made his way over to the wreckage.
The ambulance people were still helping the pilot. I remember being relieved that a doctor was present, and a new hope had come over the first responders on the scene. "We can save him now!" I thought to myself.

The doctor walked up to the pilot who was still alive and said, "He's dead." We all looked at the doctor in total astonishment. The patient was in fact alive.

I was no longer a witness to the pilot's care at this point. During this entire time, I didn't see that there was another plane involved. Both planes clipped each other's wings each other in midair. The other plane had crashed about 100 yards from the burning wreck. This plane didn't catch fire. It had the same effect as the first plane I encountered. That pilot crashed and broke almost every bone in his body. The way that pilot ended up after he crashed, put him in full view of his friend burning alive in the other plane.

He was hysterical when I showed up to his plane. It took us about 40 minutes to get him out of what remained of his small plane.

Just when things could not get worse, it did. A very dangerous lighting storm rolled over the entire scene. It was not your usual lightning storm. Lighting was hitting the ground all around us. We all knew we may get hit, but we kept going anyway. The risk was worth the gain in our minds. It was all a very strange anomaly.

I provided a police escort for the ambulance that took my original patient off the base. The New York state troopers took it from there all the way to the hospital. It saved valuable seconds for them when they got to the emergency room. The pilot who was burned, was a remarkably strong man. He survived the transport to hospital and survived a helicopter transport to a burn center. He finally expired 5 hours after the crash. At least we got him 5 hours more of life.

Chapter 33

PRESS RELEASES

Barry Donadio conducts book signing.
April 17th 2015
Ocean City, Maryland

Author Barry Donadio gave away free signed copies of his book at his recent book signing in Ocean City, Maryland.

Barry Donadio was one of the first responding emergency medical technicians to the TWA Flight 800 tragedy. All 230 persons on board died on the night of July 17th, 1996. In his book, he describes what he encountered on the evening of the crash.

In 2002, Barry Donadio obtained a position at the White House while serving in the U.S. Secret Service. After serving over 10 years of Government service, he opened a private security and investigation firm named "Public Security LLC".

Donadio stated that he would be writing more books in the future that would be of interest to the public.

Author Donadio donates 475 books
January 16th 2016

Barry Donadio of Chester donated 475 free copies of his book in January 2016. The eBooks were donated globally to commemorate the 20th anniversary of the TWA Flight 800 crash that occurred on July 17, 1996. Barry Donadio's book is called "TWA Flight 800 First Responder Witness Account."

At the time of the crash, Donadio was a 25-year-old emergency medical technician who responded to the scene. It is the only book on the market that was written by someone who was at the scene of the rescue operations. The book was originally released Sept. 16, 2013, and it describes the events that unfolded on the night of the tragedy.

Donadio also was employed as an U.S. Air Force Security Police officer at the same military base that some people blame for shooting down the plane (The 106th Rescue Wing at Gabreski Airbase, Westhampton Beach, NY). He later became an USAF security police investigator and a SWAT team leader at that same unit. In 2002, he moved to Maryland after taking a position at the White House with the U.S. Secret Service.

Donadio does not comment as to why the plane crashed, but he said, "This account offers a look inside the Coast Guard station.

"It offers some clues that may support your opinion as to what may have truly happened to the plane and why it may have crashed."

He went on to say, "I have included descriptions of the some of the victims' fates, as well as other interesting anomalies that I observed on that evening."

Included in the book, are some of his experiences before and after the crash that he responded to as a firefighter/EMT on Long Island.

Donadio plans to meet with the families of victims of the crash and attend memorial services in New York on July 16, 2016

Barry Donadio reminisces of the TWA Flight 800 Disaster 19 Years Ago July 16th, 2015

Still fresh in his mind, July 16th, 2015, is the 19-year anniversary of the TWA Flight 800 tragedy.

On that night, Barry Donadio responded to help the victims of TWA Flight 800 as an emergency medical technician. First responders on the scene, originally thought there were survivors that evening. Unfortunately, that was not the case.

Read about what he witnessed that evening and some other interesting facts and events. He also shared in his book some experiences that he encountered as a firefighter on Long Island in the 1990s

In honor of the victims of TWA Flight 800, he privately prayed for them.

Donadio recently authorized the sale of his book in kindle version on Amazon.

Barry Donadio recalls the TWA Flight 800 on the 20-year anniversary of the crash
July, 2016

Donadio joins TWA Flight 800 family members in prayer at a memorial to the victims in East Moriches, New York

My response to the crash began from a tiny ambulance garage in New York. I was an Emergency Medical Technician with the East Moriches community volunteer ambulance. From that ambulance garage, we responded to the East Moriches Coast Guard station. Once there, we first though that we would be tending to survivors. As boats brought the bodies of the victims to the Coast Guard station, we began to realize the horrible reality. There was that not even one person that survived the crash. Death did not discriminate on that terrible night. Men, women, and children of all ages perished. It did not matter what race or religion they were; they were all taken that night without prejudice.

Barry Donadio with TWA Flight 800 families in East Moriches, New York
July 1996

Barry Donadio briefs TWA flight 800 families at Moriches Coast Guard station on 20th anniversary July 17th 2016
East Moriches, New York

Barry Donadio led events commemorating the 20-year anniversary of the downing of TWA Flight 800 on Long Island. The controversial crash occurred on July 17th, 1996. There are still many people with questions as to why the plane crashed. Most people were attending events to remember their loved ones and friends.

Mr. Donadio authored the book "TWA Flight 800 First Responder Witness Account". It was released in September 2013 and has been gaining more interest. The book is about his account of the evening the plane went down. He was an Emergency Medical Technician that responded to the scene of the rescue operations.

Donadio stated: "I felt that it was important to remember the victims of the tragedy on the 20th anniversary. I was happy to meet families of some of the victims. We turned the 20th anniversary of a horrible event, into a positive day for all those who attended."

Mr. Donadio led victims' families to the TWA Flight 800 Memorial in Shirley, New York as well as the TWA Flight 800 Memorials in East Moriches New York. With the cooperation of the U.S. Coast Guard Station in Moriches, he led the group to the Coast Guard station. The group was able to access the station while Mr. Donadio explained to the group what happened there on the night of July 17th, 1996.

Donadio gives away dozens of copies of his book to TWA flight 800 families
July 17th 2016
New York

Barry Donadio gave away scores of his book to families and friends of the victims of the TWA Flight 800 crash on July 17th, 2016.

Mr. Donadio led events commemorating the 20-year anniversary of the downing of TWA Flight 800 on Long Island. The controversial crash occurred on July 17th, 1996. There are still many people with questions as to why the plane crashed. Most people were attending events to remember their loved ones and friends.

Mr. Donadio authored the book "TWA Flight 800 First Responder Witness Account". It was released in September 2013 and has been gaining more interest. The book is about his account of the evening the plane went down. He was an emergency medical technician that responded to the scene of the rescue operations.

Donadio stated " I felt that it was important to remember the victims of the tragedy on the 20th anniversary. I was happy to meet families of some of the victims. We turned the 20th anniversary of a horrible event, into a positive day for all those who attended."

Mr. Donadio led victims' families to the TWA Flight 800 memorial in Shirley, New York as well as the TWA Flight 800 memorials in East Moriches New York. With the cooperation of the U.S. Coast Guard Station in Moriches, he led the group to the Coast Guard station. The group was able to access the station while Mr. Donadio explained to the group what happened there on the night of July 17th 1996.

10 Things you didn't know about Barry Donadio's first book about TWA Flight 800
August 16th, 2019

Here are 10 things you never knew about Barry Donadio's First Book "TWA Flight 800 First Responder Witness Account". This may shock you.

1. He waited 17 years to publish it

Donadio spent his entire career in U.S. Government service in some way or another. Whether it was in the military or in the United State Secret Service, he always served in positions that did not permit him to release a book about his experiences. On June 28th, 2013, Donadio made a career change when he went into the private sector. This move opened the door for him to publish his first book.

2. He had to have the book censored and approved by the U.S Government prior to being published.

Because Donadio held one of the highest security clearances that you can obtain in the United States, he is obligated to submit anything he writes to the U.S. Government for potential censorship. This is due to the knowledge of a broad spectrum of government top secret information that needs to be protected.

3. The original transcript was stored in a file only to be opened after his death.

Prior to publishing his book, Donadio had left his witness account with his will and other papers in the case he died. Donadio knew that he was a part of a mysterious national event that would have many questions asked about it for decades. Being that he was at the incident, he felt he should pass his account to his family.

4. He went to the Alamo and he consulted about publishing his book with Dr. Bruce Winders, the curator of the Alamo.

Donadio travelled to San Antonio to consult with the very respected Dr. Bruce Winders who is the curator of the Alamo. Texas was always a special place for Donadio because he had lived in Galveston with his mother in 1975 for about a year. He visited the Alamo for the first time during that period and had since been intrigued by it.

5. He did not name the book

Donadio could not come up with a name for his book until he consulted with his close friend Christy Bowe of the White House Press Corps. Christy is a world class photographer and CEO of Imagecatcher News. The two met at the White House while they both worked there. They still maintain a close friendship today.

6. He does not offer an opinion as to why the plane crashed.

Donadio never speaks about why the plane crashed and offers an opinion on the matter. When he is put on the spot and asked why the plane crashed, he states: "I don't talk about why the plane crashed". This could be due to the obligations of the confidentiality agreements he signed with the government when he was employed with the military or the U.S. Secret Service. Is it that he could know why the plane crashed but he is concerned with potential repercussions? We may never know.

7. He does not make any bold claim to have partaken in any heroic actions during the incident.

Donadio is very open about his experience on the night of the incident. He makes no claim to being a hero or doing much of anything during his response to the incident. He was mostly an observer on that evening because he had no live patients to attend to as an Emergency Medical Technician on the scene. Unfortunately, all the passengers of the plane were deceased by the time they arrived where Donadio was standing by to help them.

8. He is the only person that has written a book about the crash that was there on the evening it crashed.

As of today, Donadio is the only one that we know of that wrote a book about the TWA Flt. 800 crash that was there that evening. This gives an insight of small details that occurred during the terrible evening. Many other works that have been written about the crash are highly opinionated and some are even fictional.

9. His account of the injuries inflicted on the victims of the crash differs from newspaper accounts.

If you research public information regarding how the passengers of TWA Flight 800 died, you will find many references of burned bodies. Donadio, however makes no mention of bodies that he observed having any burns or any being burned beyond recognition. This adds to the conspiracy theory supporters' point of view.

10. He wrote half of the book while sitting at his wife's deathbed.

"Donadio is only now opening up about speaking about the loss of his wife " Alexandra Catalina Donadio April 17th, 2014. Just when he began writing his book, tragedy struck in June of 2013. His wife underwent a medical procedure that took an unexpected turn leaving her in a coma for 9 months. Donadio was left caring for his 2 young daughters during the ordeal. He stayed by his wife's bedside for the entire 9 months until she died in April of 2014. It was during the worst time in his life that he worked on the book at his wife's hospital bedside.

Donadio's book TWA Flight 800 First Responder Witness Account" can be purchased on amazon.com

Barry Donadio commemorating 25th anniversary of TWA Flight 800 Downing with book signing.
July 16th, 2021

Celebrity Author Barry Donadio will have a public book signing event in Bohemia, New York on July 16th 2021 at 6pm at the La Quinta Inn located at 10 Aero Road, Bohemia, New York.

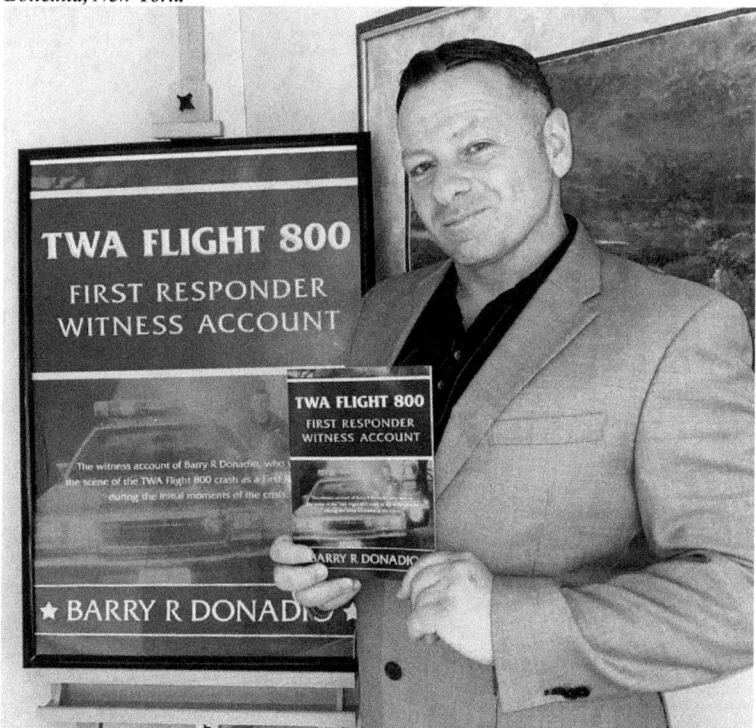

Barry Donadio July 16th 2021 book signing, Bohemia, New York

Barry Donadio will have a public book signing event in Bohemia, New York on July 16th, 2021, at 6pm at the La Quinta Inn located at 10 Aero Road, Bohemia, New York. Celebrity Author Barry Donadio will be conducting a book signing for his 1st published book "TWA Flight 800 First Responder Witness Account."

There will also be photo opportunities with the author. Barry Donadio gained fame when he published his book "TWA Flight 800 First Responder Witness Account" in September of 2013. Since then, he has been busy when he entered politics and by leading his private security firm. He has also sanctioned himself as an advocate for military veterans, and first responders.

This is the only book on the market that was written by someone who was at the scene of the crash of TWA Flight 800 on July 17th, 1996. Barry Donadio was one of the first responding Emergency Medical Technicians that responding to the disaster. This never released witness account of the events that unfolded on the night of July 17th, 1996. Barry Donadio was a 25-year-old Emergency Medical Technician that responded to the TWA Flight 800 Crash. He was a member of the local East Moriches, New York ambulance that responded to the disaster on that fateful evening.

The interesting fact is that Barry Donadio was also employed as a USAF Security Police Officer at the same military base that some circles blame for shooting down the plane (The 106th Rescue Wing at Gabreski ANG Base, Westhampton Beach, NY). He later became a USAF Security Police Investigator at that same unit. In 2002, he obtained a position in the United States Secret Service at the White House. He served the Bush and Obama administrations.

This account offers a look inside the Coast Guard station at East Moriches, where the victims of TWA Flt. 800 were brought that evening.

It offers some clues that may support your opinion as to what may have truly happened to the plane and why it may have crashed. Descriptions of the some of the victim's fates are included in the account as well as other interesting anomalies that were observed on that evening. Not for persons under the age of 18 years old. The witness account has undergone United States Government censorship, but the author documents were in the account that censorships took place. Donadio also includes in this book other experiences that he witnessed before the TWA Flight 800 crash and after the event.

Author Barry Donadio to hold book signing in Holtsville, New York
July 16th, 2022

Celebrity Author Barry Donadio will be conducting a book signing. The event will take place on July 16th 2022 from 7pm to 9pm at the Holiday Inn located at 1730 North Ocean Ave., Holtsville, New York 11742. All members of the public are welcome to attend and meet Barry Donadio.

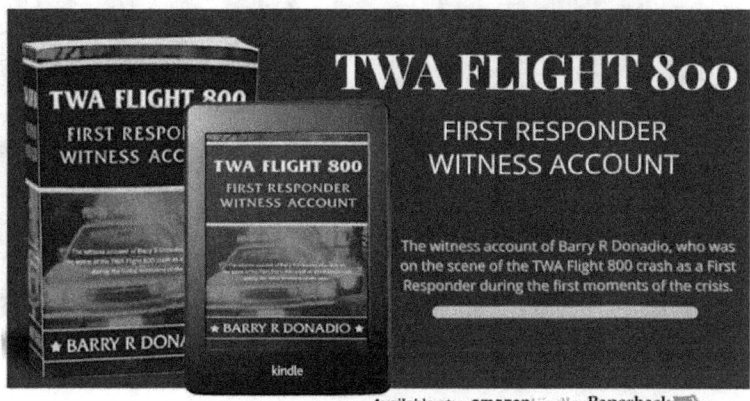

Donadio gained fame when he published his book **"TWA Flight 800 First Responder Witness Account"** in September of 2013. Since then, he has been busy when he entered politics and by leading his private security firm. He has also sanctioned himself as an advocate for military veterans, first responders and he is vocal with his support of the second amendment.

Donadio's book is the only book on the market that was written by someone who was at the scene of the crash of TWA Flight 800 on July 17th, 1996. Barry Donadio was one of the first responding Emergency Medical Technicians that responding to the disaster. This never released witness account of the events that unfolded on the night of July 17th, 1996.

He was a 25-year-old emergency medical technician that responded to the TWA Flight 800 Crash. He was a member of the local East Moriches, New York ambulance that responded to the disaster on that fateful evening.

The interesting fact is that Barry Donadio was also employed as a USAF Security Police Officer at the same military base that some circles blame for shooting down the plane (The 106th Rescue Wing at Gabreski ANG Base, Westhampton Beach, NY). He later became a USAF Security Police Investigator at that same unit.

In 2002, he obtained a position in the United States Secret Service at the White House. He served the Bush and Obama administrations. This account offers a look inside the Coast Guard Station at East Moriches, where the victims of TWA Flt. 800 were brought that evening. It offers some clues that may support your opinion as to what may have truly happened to the plane and why it may have crashed. Donadio includes in the book many of his experiences as a Firefighter on Long Island leading up to the plane crash.

Descriptions of the some of the victim's fates are included in the account as well as other interesting anomalies that were observed on that evening. Not for persons under the age of 18 years old.
The witness account has undergone United States Government censorship, but the author documents were in the account that censorships took place.

NOTE: This book does not offer an opinion or theory for the reason why the aircraft crashed. It is written as an impartial witness account.

Barry Donadio is a celebrity author and native of Bay Shore, New York. He led an honorable career in the Volunteer Ambulance Service, Volunteer Fire Department, the military, law enforcement, and the United States Secret Service. He was assigned to the White House to protect Presidents Bush and Obama. He also served in multiple middle Eastern war zones during his career. In 2013, he authored the book " TWA Flight 800 First Responder Witness Account". This is his account describing his actions during the rescue of TWA Flight 800 on July 17th, 1996. In 2014, he was elected to the Queen Anne's County Republican Central Committee in Maryland. He successfully completed his 4-year term. January 2017, he was appointed the Sergeant at Arms of the Maryland Republican Party. As of January1st 2023, he still serves as the Sgt. at Arms of the MDGOP. Donadio continues to also serve as the Founder and President of Public Security LLC. This firm conducts high-risk private security and investigations. It also provides protection to clients in Maryland and New York. Public Security LLC provides executive protection for numerous political figures, celebrities, and wealthy persons. Donadio is a prestigious Private Detective that handles cases requiring strict trust and confidentiality. Donadio published his second book "That Day When Hell Froze Over" on August 17th, 2019.

Donadio received multiple military medals during his military service which included the Armed Forces Expeditionary Medal and the Air Force Commendation Medal among others.

On June 24, 2019 Barry Donadio was awarded the Global War on Terrorism Service Medal for his service while still in the military back in 2002.

On March 30th, 2022 Barry Donadio was awarded New York State's Medal For Merit by the Division of Military and Naval Affairs 20 years after he served in the military. The medal commemorates his honorable service in the Armed Forces and the State of New York.

On May 18, 2022, Barry Donadio was awarded New York State's Conspicuous Service Star medal by New York Gov. Kathy Hochul. The governor presented the medal to Donadio on behalf of representatives in the New York legislature 20 years after he served in the military. The medal commemorates his honorable service in the Armed Forces and the State of New York.

Donadio still serves and will always serve the people of the United States of America.

www.ingramcontent.com/pod-product-compliance
Lightning Source LLC
LaVergne TN
LVHW051835080426
835512LV00018B/2900